THE MEANING OF MEANINGLESSNESS

The Meaning
of
Meaninglessness

by

GENE BLOCKER

0142771

MARTINUS NIJHOFF / THE HAGUE / 1974

83691

For Margaret and Harry

© 1974 by Martinus Nijhoff, The Hague, Netherlands
*All rights reserved, including the right to translate or to
reproduce this book or parts thereof in any form*

ISBN 90 247 1595 4

PRINTED IN BELGIUM

TABLE OF CONTENTS

INTRODUCTION   IX

Chapter 1. THE DIVERSITY OF MEANING   1

Chapter 2. THE UNITY OF MEANING   33

Chapter 3. MEANING AND MEANINGLESSNESS   73

Chapter 4. THE TRAGIC SENSE OF MEANINGLESSNESS   102

Chapter 5. BACK TO SQUARE ONE   114

BIBLIOGRAPHY   143

INDEX   145

014277/

83091

014877

83901

Once a boy met a girl. They agreed to a race. The boy chased the girl from dawn to salfana, 2 p.m. prayers. They prayed and rested. The boy then drove the girl from salfana to lansara, 5 p.m. prayers. By this time the boy was bleeding and vomiting blood. He fell on the ground. The girl turned back and picked him up.

What happened? asked the boy. You are a girl,
I am a man. I chase you from morning
till night and yet you cannot be held.

You are a foolish boy!
I agree to your word and you enter into
an agreement with me without asking my name.
You just chase me.
You are very foolish.
You trouble yourself unnecessarily.

Girl, what is your name?

My name is Duniya. I am the World.
No one can hold the world.
You can chase the world until you are tired,
until your hands are bleeding.
From the time you are a small child,
from the time you grow and learn the kuran,
from the time you pass through circumcision
until your hair grows white and your mouth
is collapsed and toothless, you may chase the world.
But no one will hold Duniya. Now you are a man.

You have a wife of your own. Yet you follow me
without asking my name. The world is wide and
long. If you go to the right, those on the left
will not know you. If you go to the left, those
on the right will not know you. If you go up
the people below will not know you. If you go
down the people above will not know you.
Duniya is wide. Duniya is long.
My name is Do What You Are Able. Although
you try, you cannot win the world. The world will
win you … . Duniya ita tola.

(A Mandingo tale narrated by Sara Madi Dumbuya, 28/2/68, Port
Loko, Sierra Leone, West Africa and translated by Mary Howard.)

INTRODUCTION

What does "meaningless" mean? On the one hand, it signifies simply the absence or lack of meaning. "Zabool" is meaningless just because it doesn't happen to mean anything. "Green flees timelessly" is meaningless, despite a certain semblance of sense, because it runs afoul of certain fundamental rules of linguistic construction. On the other hand, "meaningless" characterizes that peculiar psychological state of dread and anxiety much discussed, if not discovered, by the French shortly after the Second World War. The first is primarily linguistic, focusing attention on emotionally neutral questions of linguistic meaning. The second is nonlinguistic, indicating a painful probing of the social psychology of an era, a clinical and literary analysis of 20th century Romanticism. On the one hand, a job for the professional philosopher; on the other hand, a task for the literary critic and the social historian.

Is any useful purpose served in trying to combine these two, very different concerns? As the title of this book suggests, I think there is. In what follows I try to show that there is an important connection between linguistic meaning and the feeling of nausea, dread and absurdity described by the Existentialists, and that the latter constitutes an important, though neglected field for the study of meaning, whether linguistic or otherwise. Indeed, I will argue that linguistic meaning can be properly understood only in the broader context of this nonlinguistic meaning. In this sense, "the meaning of meaninglessness" suggests a fundamental reexamination of the "meaning of *meaning*."

There is, of course, a very widespread contemporary use of words like "meaninglessness" and "absurdity" on the part of critics, literary historians, sociologists, and the like, for describing a mass sociohistorical, psychological fact of our times. Yet it has never been made sufficiently clear what this means. The feelings of nausea, claustro-phobia, density and vertigo have been carefully and sensitively described, but the sense in which these psychological moods either are, or contribute to, a *loss of meaning* is far from being satisfactorily explained.

As a result, some writers, those in the above mentioned group, use these terms as though they required no explanation, in some cases arguing that, being feelings, such things cannot be explained but must be experienced or "lived through" in order to be understood. This provides the perfect foil for a second group of writers, this time the "analytic" philosophers, who, for this very reason, dismiss all such talk as nonsense, that is, a misuse of the term "meaning." Meaning, they say, has to do with units of language, words, sentences, etc.; that the *world* should be meaningful or that *life* could be meaning-less is simply a confusion of language, simply a misunderstanding of what we mean by "meaning."

My own aim is philosophical, though not narrowly so. I intend to provide a conceptual analysis which is at once a reasonably rigorous philosophical account of meaninglessness in its relation to various kinds and senses of meaning, but which is at the same time as true to the modern feeling of meaninglessness and absurdity as a con-ceptual analysis can be to its subject matter. Should this help to bridge the "credibility gap" between English-speaking "analytic" philosophers and their Continental counterparts, the Phenom-enologists and the Existentialists, I would be very pleased, but this is not my primary objective.

Admittedly, the task I am outlining is not an easy one; we tend to approach questions of meaning and meaninglessness from one of several fixed points of view. The traditional account of meaning, from Hobbes to Richards, is narrowly intellectual, while the dissenting Romantic tradition, from Coleridge to Ionesco, tends to the opposite, anti-intellectual side of the same coin. Within the framework of these historical perspectives, the position I wish to develop would thus seem to be "caught between a rock and a hard place", to vary the usual classical allusion. For this reason, we will have to break new ground in our approach to the theory of meaning, not without acknowledging, however, a considerable debt to the pioneering work of Wittgenstein and Heidegger.

We will want to throw open the question of meaning as widely as possible at first, merely listing and describing a surprising variety of different senses and uses of "meaning" and "meaningless," before trying to sift out the larger strands or kinds of meaning to see how they are related to one another. These will include, besides linguistic meaning, meaning in the sense of purpose or intention, meaning as the systematic interrelatedness of parts within a whole, and the recognition of something as the kind of thing which it is, which I will call "being-as," a philosophical play on the term "seeing-as." The lack of any one of these, with the exception of linguistic meaning, will result in the kind of meaninglessness described by the Existentialists. I will try to push my analysis further and say that in the broadest sense meaning is a kind of interpretation, or projection thrown upon the world, the recognition of which is a sense of meaninglessness. This points to a curiously paradoxical relationship between meaning and meaninglessness which is the real subject of the book, adding a further dimension to "the meaning of meaninglessness." For, in one sense, if meaning is a kind of projection and the recognition of projection is a sense of meaninglessness, then the sense of meaninglessness rests squarely on the nature of meaning. Looking at it the other way, if meaning is only possible by a kind of projection which is regarded as meaningless, then, equally, meaning rests on the conditions of meaninglessness. Indeed, the irony can be brought out more forcefully. If meaninglessness is the recognition of the interpreted, or projective nature of meaning, then meaninglessness, in one sense at least, is simply the recognition of the nature of meaning. Thus, an analysis of meaning seems to dissolve into a discussion of meaninglessness, while meaninglessness, on the other hand, dialectically reduces to a kind of meaning. But this is very strange. How can the recognition of the nature of meaning lead to, or constitute, the feeling of meaninglessness? How can projection be both a necessary condition for meaning and also a necessary condition for meaninglessness?

The point is not to gloat over these fine ironies, but to provide some initial suggestion of the riches to be unpacked from the deeply ambiguous interrelatedness of meaning and meaninglessness. In one sense "meaning" signifies a kind of projection we confer upon things, but in another sense, it signifies just the opposite. It is often said, for example, that meaning is simply an interpretation we assign to things, that things *don't* have the meanings we thought they had. But this implies that meaning is *not* projection, but something inherent in and indentical with the things themselves. On the one hand we recognize that meaning is a conventional designation, not an inherent feature in the world; on the other hand we insist that meaning must be an ingredient in the real nature of the thing itself without which that thing is meaningless. While recognition of the interpretive, "projection" character of meaning reinforces the first sense of meaning (projection), it is diametrically opposed to the second (nonprojection) sense of meaning. Thus, it follows from this preliminary analysis that meaninglessness is not absolutely opposed to meaning, as a superficial logical analysis would suggest. Meaninglessness is fully compatible with meaning in the sense of projection; it is only incompatible with a nonprojective sense of meaning which simply identifies meaning with reality. But this identification is highly suspect, as we will see, and this suggests that resolving the tragic modern sense of meaninglessness is primarily the clearing away of a dust we have raised ourselves (an allusion to Zen Buddhism, which we will discuss in Chapter 5, as well as to Berkeley), the dust being the nonprojective sense of meaning.

Each of these, for the moment, cryptic statements indicates a major theme to be developed in subsequent chapters. Thus, for example, Chapter 3 is an exploration of the idea that, historically, the search for meaning has led to a sense of meaninglessness, that, paradoxically, a necessary condition for the tragic modern sense of meaninglessness is a naive objectivist, or nonprojective, sense of meaning. This is exemplified in a number of different ways; in the scientist's struggle to get to the bottom of things (which results in a "neutralization of nature"), in the philosopher's search into the conditions of truth and meaning, in the phenomenon Heidegger calls "fallenness," and in the inevitable frustration, described by the mystic, of trying to hold the world in a fishnet of concepts. As Heidegger points out, we lose ourselves in a world of things; naively we are absorbed in a "real" world of nonprojective, "objective" meaning. This is what makes possible a meaningful "world," but it is also the first step towards a sense of meaninglessness since this absorption conceals the fact that a meaningful world is a human accomplishment, a projection of man's self onto the world. The encroachment of meaninglessness is held at bay only by "bad faith," throwing ourselves ever more desparately into the acquisition and enjoyment of things which themselves become less and less meaningful. But this only masks the problem, driving it deeper. Thus, the underlying uneasiness, the fear of waking up to meaninglessness becomes more acute, more out in the open. We try to shore up a dwindling sense of a meaningful world of everyday experience by considerations of an ultimate, transcendent guarantee of meaning. But this, too, has just the opposite effect, making us more and more conscious that there *is* no absolute, objective meaning.

Thus, a necessary condition for the sense of meaninglessness is a naive objectivist, nonprojective sense of meaning. This accounts for the tragic Existentialist sense of meaninglessness discussed in Chapter 4, the response to which is one of dread, anguish, and nausea. This tragic sense of meaninglessness is the product of *two* contradictory senses of meaning, projective and nonprojective. There is nothing tragic simply in the realization that meaning is projection; this becomes tragic only where it means, as it does for many of us in the 20th century, that meaning is *not nonprojective*. It is only by contrast with the supposed *ideal* of nonprojective meaning that the realization that meaning is a form of projection has the tragic consequences it has for many people today. Without this ideal, meaninglessness would simply be the realization that the meaningful world of everyday experience is an interpreted world, a human accomplishment. Without the nonprojective ideal of meaning, this is what *constitutes* a meaningful world, not what *denies* meaning to that world. This, in turn, helps explain the fact that in certain Eastern philosophies, notably Zen Buddhism, there is a completely different response to meaninglessness. In Zen meaninglessness is greeted with a sense of joy and relief, and this is primarily because the Zen experience of meaninglessness is not conditioned by a pining after an absolute, nonprojective sense of meaning.

In Chapter 5 I explore the possibility of this positive response to meaninglessness. Meaninglessness now becomes the awareness that we must project meaning in order to achieve a coherent, everyday world, along with the realization that a refusal to acknowledge this projection is ultimately self-frustrating and fraught with anxiety and unhappiness. There is no attempt to block projection; indeed the realization is that projection is necessary for the meaningful world of everyday experience. What must be held in check is the idea that projection falls short of some imaginary goal of nonprojective meaning. Thus, it is not projection which is at fault, but this ideal of nonprojective meaning. This is a development of our initial suggestion that meaninglessness is not necessarily incompatible with meaning. We project meaning and thus enjoy the meaningful world of everyday experience; but we are aware at the same time that we are projecting, and this is a form of meaninglessness. Because *this* sense of meaninglessness abandons completely the idea of a non-projective meaning, both as an ideal and as a possibility, it cuts itself off from the frustrations, anxieties, and misery attached to the ideal of nonprojective meaning, and thus achieves a kind of solution to the modern problem of meaninglessness.

Putting the point more simply and more crudely, there are two main senses of meaningfulness, the naive objectivist, nonprojection ideal of meaning which simply identifies meaning with reality, and the sense of living in a coherent and comprehensible everyday world. There are equally two corresponding senses of meaninglessness, the realization and acceptance of the fact that meaning is a form of projection or human achievement, and the loss of a comprehensible "world." The traditional view holds that meaningfulness in the sense of "having a world" is incompatible with meaninglessness in the sense of the realization of projection. This determines traditional attitudes toward projection—fending it off at all costs, or, where this is impossible, embracing meaninglessness as its only alternative. My position is that the two are fully compatible, that one can project meaning *knowing* that one is projecting, just as one can walk or sing knowing that one is walking or singing. In this sense, meaninglessness is not the tragic loss of the naive objectivist ideal of meaning, but the realization that this is a false and destructive ideal which is itself a form of projection differing from other sorts of projection only in its blind self-opaqueness. In other words, not only is the nonprojective identification of meaning with reality *not essential* to a coherent, meaningful world; it leads instead to the *loss* of such a world. The realization of projection is not, then, synonymous with the loss of a "world;" the fact that historically the one has led to the other is based on a mistaken notion of meaning. It is not projection, but the nonprojection sense of meaning which is responsible for this loss of a meaningful world. The central theme in my analysis is the irony that meaninglessness in a truly tragic sense is the product of the traditional concept of meaningfulness. Thus, my analysis requires jettisoning the nonprojective identification of meaning with reality, an idea so deeply embedded in our ordinary ways of thinking that it is difficult even to catch sight of it, much less consider alternatives to it.

Seen in this light, the thesis I will develop may be regarded as somewhat revolutionary, arguing as it does that the traditional ideal of meaning is not only mistaken and inconsistent, but also undesirable in the extreme, and urging a complete revaluation of our emotional response to meaninglessness. My analysis will also require a radical alteration of our concept of projection. Projection, I will argue, is *not* the source of meaninglessness in the genuinely tragic sense of the loss of a coherent world, as the traditional analysis insists, but on the contrary, the indispensable foundation for the meaningful, coherent world of ordinary experience.

Thus, the question of the "meaning of meaninglessness" concerns not only a clarification of the concept of meaninglessness, though this will be our first task. It is also, and primarily, an exploration of the dialectical relationship between meaning and meaninglessness, the result of which should be to put our understanding of meaning on a new and more sound footing.

CHAPTER 1

THE DIVERSITY OF MEANING

Clearly, there are many senses of "meaning" other than the standard linguistic signification of words and sentences; the question is whether these nonlinguistic senses are important for a philosophical account of meaning. Sign-signification theorists, like I. A. Richards, think they are; analytic philosophers, like William Alston, think they are not. In the *Encyclopedia of Philosophy* Alston offers the following list of different uses of "mean" and "meaning," only one of which, the last, is linguistic.

I mean to help him if I can.
The passage of this bill will mean the end of second-class citizenship.
Once again, life has meaning for me.
What is the meaning of this!?
Keep off the grass. This means you.
Procrastination means putting things off.[1]

Having acknowledged this diversity, he goes on to say that philosophy is concerned only with the last, to which the rest of the article is devoted.

Alston's specification of different senses of meaning is not intended as a classification, though it clearly presupposes one; he deliberately avoids any mention or description of *what* sense each of these entries is supposed to be an example. This is probably in reaction to the tendency in earlier semantic accounts, like that of Richards, of prescribing in advance certain *a priori* categories which all examples were presumed, or made to fit. Nonetheless, Richards' early attempt at classification is full of interesting suggestions and provides a

---

[1] *Encyclopedia of Philosophy*, Paul Edwards (ed.), London: Collier and Macmillan, Ltd., 1967.

better grasp of the range of meanings than Alston's studied anti-classification stance. In *The Meaning of Meaning* (to which the title of this book bears a not inconsequential resemblance) Richards distinguishes eight main senses of "meaning," [2] for which I will suggest examples from ordinary speech.

1) Essence: e.g., What is the meaning of baptism (... of totalitarianism, of life)?

2) Attitude projected into something: e.g., What meaning do you attach to this line?

3) Event intended: e.g., Do you mean to go now?

4) The place of X in a system: e.g., What does it mean when the priest sprinkles the water (... when the referee raises his arms)?

5) Practical consequences of X: e.g., The passage of this bill will mean the end of second-class citizenship.

6) Emotion aroused by X: e.g., Money means little to me. Once again life has meaning for me.

7) What a thing suggests by association: e.g., Buzzing means bees and bees mean honey.

8) The natural connection between things: e.g., Dark clouds mean rain.

Not all of these are on a par. Numbers 1 and 2 suggest theories rather than types of meaning, as supplied by 3 through 8. Taken together, however, the last five examples do indicate another theory of meaning which Richards goes on to develop. This is the positivist or objectivist theory derived from 7 and 8 in which the emphasis is placed on the natural or conventional relation of one object to another, playing down, in other words, the intentional or "subjective" side of meaning.

Richards tries to reduce all kinds of meaning to one basic kind, while Alston, in effect, denies any discernible pattern in the profusion of different uses of "meaning." These may be said to represent two extremes in recent theories of meaning. Perhaps the most philosophically impartial account of the different senses of meaning is to be found in any of a half dozen reputable English and American dictionaries, of which the following, taken largely from the *Oxford English Dictionary*, is a synthesis.

---

[2] Richards, I. A. and Ogden, C. K., *The Meaning of Meaning*, London: Routledge and Kegan Paul, 1956.

MEAN

1) to intend (have in mind)
   I mean to help him if I can.
   Do you mean to go now?
   No malice we mente. (1490)
   He meant (for) you to stay.
   (He) menit to subvert the lawis. (Reg. Privy Council Scotland, 1567)
   You only mean to haunt me! (Goldsmith, 1773)
   What do you mean bursting in on me like that?
   What is the meaning of this?
   He meant you no harm.
   He means mischief.
   I mean business.

2) to design a thing for a definite purpose
   Warre not ment against (them) (Dons, 1560)
   When greate griefes to me he ment (Sidney, 1580)
   (Fate) should hide ... all that's meant me (Browning, 1842)
   He meant it to be used as (for) a footstool.
   It was meant (to be used) as (for) a footstool.
   What is Man meant to do upon this earth? What is the meaning of life?
   He was meant for (to be) a soldier.

3) to intend a remark to have a particular reference
   Keep off the grass. This means you.
   Was that meant at (to, of) him?
   I mean his father.
   When you spoke just now of one of your more promising students, did you mean Jonathan?

4) to intend to convey a thought by a certain form of speech
   Understand the sense in which it is meant.
   The Act doesn't literally mean what it says.
   He meant more than met the ear.
   I mean that he is stingy.

5) to be well-, or ill-, intentioned
   He means well.
   He wolde ... mene wel to me. (Chaucer)

6) standard signification of a word, phrase, sentence
   What does "ja" mean?
   Procrastination means putting things off.
7) leads to, effects, or is associated, or connected with
   Money means happiness.
   Dark clouds mean rain.
   The passage of this bill will mean the end of second-class citizenship.
   Buzzing means bees and bees mean honey.
8) to have a specified degree of importance to someone
   Money means little to me.
   Once again life has meaning for me.
   She means a lot (the world) to me.
   Little things mean a lot.

MEANING

1) intention, purpose
   What is the meaning of this (intrusion)?
2) that which is intended to be (or actually is) expressed or conveyed
   a) by language
      There was no meaning to (in) his words.
      This word has different meanings.
      We must distinguish the meaning of a statement from its truth. (Butler)
      Don't ask for the meaning, ask for the use. (Wittgenstein)
   b) by dreams, symbols, and other phenomena
      The Greeks sought the meaning of their myths.
      He saw a vision and sought its meaning.
      What is the meaning of the sacrament?
3) having good or ill intentions
   His address was well-meaning.
4) that which conveys or expresses meaning or thought or is emotionally important to someone
   a meaning look (cf., a meaningful look)
   a meaning smile (cf., a meaningless smile)
   a look full of meaning (Kingsley)
   Life again has meaning for me.

MEANINGLESS; lacking meaning

meaningless definitions (Locke)
meaningless remarks (Lamb to Coleridge)
meaninglessly lost (Ruskin)

MEANINGLESSNESS; state or condition of lacking meaning

meaninglessness of the veined marble (Ruskin)
It is not the monotony of life which destroys man, but its pointlessness ... its meaninglessness crushes him. (H. Drummond, 1894)

Archaic senses

MEAN

1) to lament or complain (1300-1578), cognate with "moan" and
   "bemoan"
2) to aim at in literal sense of directed motion (1470)
3) to remember (1303-1440)
4) to hold an opinion, to think, imagine (1300-1637)
5) to say, tell, mention (857-1494)
(All but number 2 form the original root in Old Anglo-Saxon,
Frisian, Dutch, German, Swedish, and Irish)

MEANING

1) intention or purpose (1385-1896)
2) remembrance (1300-1503)
3) mention (1300)
4) knowledge (1393) [3]

Perhaps my own bias will be detected in the selection of a list
which lays stress on intentional meaning, but at least I think this
can be supported both by current usage and etymology, as I will
try to show. Certainly, this is a far more complete list, including all

---

[3] *Oxford English Dictionary*, 1961; *An Etymological Dictionary of the English
Language*, Rev. Walter W. Skeat, Oxford: Clarendon Press, 1958; *Origins*, Eric
Partridge, London: Routledge and Kegan Paul, 1958; *The Oxford Dictionary of
English Etymology*, Onions (ed.), Oxford: Clarendon Press, 1966; *The Concise
Oxford Dictionary of Current English*, Fowler (ed.), Oxford: Clarendon Press,
1964; *Webster's New World Dictionary of the American Language*, New York:
The World Publishing Co., 1958.

the types found in Richards and Alston, plus a number of others not found in either.

From this philosophically neutral list we can begin to appreciate the primary importance of nonlinguistic meaning. Anticipating somewhat, it seems obvious from a cursory glance at the *Oxford English Dictionary* that both in current usage and in etymology the root and core of the modern sense of meaning is the nonlinguistic sense of intention or purpose, from which spring both the sense of being designed (for a certain purpose) and of linguistic meaning (intended by the speaker), as well as the quasi-intentional association of one thing with another (money "for the sake of" happiness, clouds "for the sake of" rain, bees "for the sake of" honey) and the purposively-described place of X in a system of things (the heart "in order to" pump the blood, the veins "in order to" carry the blood, the eye "for the purpose of" seeing).

When we turn from the classification of the different senses of "meaning" to recent discussions of meaning, we find much the same intentional, nonlinguistic story, especially in the contemporary anthropological emphasis on the intended place of an action or remark in a particular social context. Rankin, for example, invites us to consider the Wittgensteinian dictim, "the meaning is the use," in relation to the view of the descriptive anthropologists, e.g., Evans-Pritchard and Levi-Straus,

that the 'meaning' of a social form of behavior lies in its social syntax, i.e., in the functional interdependence between it and different forms of behavior within a spatio-temporal extended area.[4]

For example, an anthropologist may want to explain the meaning of the following behavior. A group of men are seated in a circle around a container of small stones. One man removes several handfuls, placing them in a separate pile. A second man then takes a smaller amount from the second pile, replacing the stones in the original container. The first man then removes a still smaller amount to the second pile, and so on, until neither man will move any more stones from one pile to the other. In order to discover the meaning of this behavior, the descriptive anthropologist will now try to find its intended place in the larger pattern of social behavior. He will note that the men belong to two families; that one of the men had

[4] Rankin, K. W., "Wittgenstein on Meaning, Understanding and Intending." *American Philosophical Quarterly*, vol. 3, no. 1, 1966, p. 3.

brought the stones, along with members of his family, to the house of the second man where the members of his family were already assembled. He will go on to observe that following this activity the men from the first man's family brought exactly the same number of bags of cowries to the house of the second man as the final number of stones in the second pile, and that shortly thereafter a ceremony took place which the anthropologist already understands as the marriage of the first man to the daughter of the second. Now the meaning of the original activity becomes clear. The men were bargaining over the "bride price," the meaning of which we have been led to understand by seeing its interdependency with other activities in the broader "social syntax." And the meaning of the bride price itself could be made more intelligible by seeing its place within the broader spectrum of tribal marriage, divorce, family life, and so on. This would make it clear, for example, that paying the bride price did not resemble so much paying the price of a cow or a sheep as a demonstration of the young man's ability to support a wife, as a token of esteem to the girl's family for having brought her up properly, as insurance against the girl's returning to her parents (in which case they would have to return the bride price), as recognition of the girl's value in the domestic economy, and so on.

Meaning, then, in one important nonlinguistic sense is functional interdependence, the intended place of X in a socially understood system of things. Knowing the meaning of X in this sense is not necessarily a form of explicit, conscious understanding as our understanding of linguistic meaning is often thought to be. An outsider to a particular society, such as our anthropologist, understands the meaning of X by seeing explicitly its relation to Y and Z, but a member of that society knows the meaning of X without this explicit understanding. He simply has a sense of being at home in this system, knowing his way around, experiencing no surprises or confusion. The system as such becomes apparent to him only if and when it begins to break down for him, or when, for example, after years of study in Europe, he sees it from an alien perspective and no longer feels completely at home or at ease in it. In other words, the native knows the meaning without understanding it *as* such.

It is on this basis that Rankin finds it necessary to distinguish functional interdependent meaning from linguistic meaning which he believes must involve an explicit understanding. What he means, I think, is that in order to know the meaning of the expression "This is an axe," I must understand explicitly and be able to explain its relation to certain situations and forms of behavior, e.g., when and where it is to be used and for what purpose and with what result, etc. But this seems very doubtful. Forms of speech can have the same conceptual opaqueness to the native speaker as other forms of behavior. It is true that most native speakers will be able to tell you what certain words mean, particularly the nouns and adjectives, and in this sense not only know the meaning but understand it *as* such, but for any speaker there will be many words and forms of speech, such as prepositions and forms of address, which he will simply know how to use but will not understand in the mannеɪ, say, of the anthropologist or the lexicographer. "But," one may object, "at least the native speaker thinks of language and units of language as *having* meaning, even if he is sometimes unable to supply that meaning, while he does *not* think of nonlinguistic things as having meaning." But this is simply false. Restricting meaning to units of language is the philosopher's narrowness, not the "plain man's." The latter finds nothing strange, or even elliptical in speaking of the meaning of one's actions or dreams, or the meaningfulness of a gesture, or the meaninglessness of an outmoded social institution. What is true in Rankin's claim is that the plain man does not normally think of the entire social system in which he lives as being "meaningful," though he can and occasionally does think of it as such. (And, of course, *we* are always in a position to say of *him* that he appears to live in a meaningful or meaningless world.)

If we think of meaning as an identity relation, as in translation, where we can *say what* the meaning of X is ("*ja*" means "yes", i.e., "*ja*" = "yes"), or in dreams where we would like to be able to specify a one-to-one relation between dream items and statable meaning items (the house *means* the womb, i.e., the house *is* the womb,) then we will probably hesitate to say that the interrelatedness of things in a social system *is* the meaning (just as philosophers have balked at saying that the meaning *is* the use, something Wittgenstein himself never actually claimed). Instead we may want to say that functional interdependency is that which makes meaning *possible*, or in terms of which we *understand* the meaning of a certain situation. This way of speaking is not objectionable, but it does not prohibit our saying that in one sense meaning *is* functional interdependency. Meaning in the sense of identity or translation is only one kind of meaning; meaning can also be said to be the interrelatedness of things in a system in a quite straightforward way. When we say the social system *has* meaning or has *lost* meaning, what do we understand it has or has lost but this interconnectedness of things? Simliarly, when we say we must understand the meaning of an action in its broader social context, what understanding of this meaning can we possibly gain but the place of X in this social context, seeing its relation to Y and Z within a whole system of relations? The point is, there *is* nothing in this case which we can express in words with which the meaning is identical. We do not say the social system has *a* meaning, which invites the question, "*what* meaning?"; we say that it has or does not have *meaning*, that it is or is not *meaningful*. The question of identity or translation is simply out of place here. There *are* important differences between linguistic meaning and other forms of meaning, due primarily to our special ability to explain linguistic meaning linguistically, but the difference is one between different forms of *meaning*, not that between meaning and something else. What lies behind our saying that functional interdependency makes meaning possible, is that this is what makes *linguistic* meaning possible. In the final analysis, as Wittgenstein has shown, linguistic meaning must be understood in terms of such nonlinguistic forms of meaning as functional interdependency.

In his article "Philosophical Anthropology and the Problem of Meaning" H. P. Rickman also criticises the exclusively linguistic approach to meaning. On Rickman's view, linguistic meaning is addressed to and presupposes an already meaningful environment interpreted from a particular human point of view. That we have and must have and can only have such an interpreted world Rickman refers to as the "human situation." What we call "the world," "environment" or "reality" is necessarily part of a meaningful world seen from a limited human perspective, and in this sense *all* knowledge is "standpoint bound," locked within the human situation. We cannot step outside this framework and see things as they are "in themselves," that is, without any meaning or perspective.[5] Even to say that knowledge is an interpretation, and therefore limited by human needs and desires, is itself an interpretation.

The difficulty in discussing this type of meaning, and one reason it has been ignored by analytic philosophers, is the conceptual barren-

---

[5] Rickman, H. P., "Philosophical Anthropology and the Problem of Meaning." *The Philosophical Quarterly*, vol. 10, 1960, pp. 13-15.

ness of saying *what* an event, action or phenomenon means. Because of the environment in which I was brought up, a chair is a "meaningful" item in my experience in a way it would not be for someone who had never seen European furniture. I see it and recognize it as something to sit on, rest in, eat on, etc. But if the chair has meaning, one could ask, what exactly does it mean? Well, nothing, or rather, as we saw earlier, nothing we consciously or explicitly understand and could put into words. This is reminiscent of the dilemma with which Marhenke used to confront his philosophy students by asking for examples of their supposed "inexpressible thoughts." The meaning does not appear *as* meaning; it consists simply in my having a "structural perceptual experience," [6] involving the recognition of the component parts. This is the type of meaning which I will call "being-as," a play on the term "seeing-as." In Wittgensteinian terms I "continuously" see the chair *as* a chair; it simply takes its place in a structured or patterned experience the whole of which is the interpreted world in which I live and move. But I would not normally *say*, "I interpret it (or see it) *as* a chair," or that it "*means* a chair," (although others may say of me, "He sees it as a chair"). Only when I shift my perspective somewhat does this "dawn on me;" [7] only when I consider it, say, from the point of view of the anthropologist or the artist do I gain an explicitly conscious awareness of the chair-aspect as such. Only then would it make sense to say, "We understand this as a piece of furniture, something to sit on, etc." For the phenomenologically oriented philosopher it is this brute familiarity of things (the identity of, or rather the failure to distinguish, meaning and reality) which makes common objects and situations conceptually opaque and which makes so difficult the philosophical task of presenting these everyday objects in a theoretically interesting and arresting light.

But whatever the difficulties in describing meaning in the sense of being-as, it is undeniable that situations, events, actions and phenomena are commonly regarded in everyday speech as meaningful or meaningless, and it would therefore seem mere laziness or philosophical timidity to eschew altogether the theoretical investigation of this important type of meaning. Besides, being-as is not an *utterly*

---

[6] *Ibid.*, p. 16.

[7] Wittgenstein, Ludwig, *Philosophical Investigations* (G. E. M. Anscombe, trans.). New York: The Macmillan Co., 1953, p. 194 ff.

sterile notion; we *can* indicate, albeit in a roundabout way, what the chair means. We can imaginatively contrast our experience with an Australian aborgine's first experience of a chair, or that of a child, who, after all, does not automatically or originally know about chairs but must gradually acquire such understanding; we could also discuss its meaning in terms of our behavioral anticipations and expectations (how oddly lacking, for example, a room would look devoid of all furniture, or how strange chairs would look hung from the walls like paintings; and so on). In this sense we *can*—and just did—put into words what the chair means, but not "just like that," just as we can, in a sense, express thoughts which "lie too deep for words," though not completely or exactly. This indicates an important ambiguity in what can and cannot be "put into words" which it will be our job to uncover in Chapter 5.

In Rickman's preliminary investigation he analyses the "meaning situation" into four basic aspects or "categories" which "represent the most important relationships through which meaning is constituted." These are (1) whole-part, (2) effecting and being affected, (3) inner-outer (in a psychological sense) and (4) means-end.[8] These categories of "being-as" contain valuable suggestions for the theory of meaning, overlapping significantly with the types of meaning already discussed. "Whole-part" is the meaning of a situation as determined by context. This corresponds with "functional interdependency" and the "place of X in a system." Consider the following situation. A man tears up a letter and throws it down on a table. The meaning of this situation obviously depends on the context in which it occurs. If the man is alone and the action is accompanied by a violent curse, we understand the action in terms of anger; if he enters B's office, tears up the letter, throws it on B's desk and stands glaring at B, we see his behavior as an act of defiance, and so on. "Affecting and being affected by" has to do with the "power" an object or situation can have on us. This corresponds to meaning as the emotion aroused by X and the natural and associative connections between things mentioned earlier. Receiving the letter means the end of a love affair, the termination of a job, an insult, etc. "Inner-outer" is our understanding of the relation between thought and expression. A man's tearing up a letter differs from a chimpanzee's in that we attribute to the former feelings or thoughts which we can

[8] Rickman, *op. cit.*, p. 16.

understand and appreciate as being appropriate to that situation. "Means-end" has to do with meaning in the sense of intention, purpose and the practical consequences of an act. In the example above, B may say, "I suppose this means you are quitting (or that you want to have it out here and now, once and for all)."

These categories are anthropological in the sense that they represent different human responses to one's environment as perceived within the human situation. Within this situation we try to make the world comprehensible by relating parts within a larger whole, by recognizing and responding to the impact of the environment on us, and so on. Language, on this view, is an articulation and classification of an already interpreted and, in the sense of being-as, meaningful world.

Another anthropological type of meaning with which other non-linguistic forms of meaning appear closely related is the purpose for which something is designed. Probably the clearest analysis of purpose and design in relation to meaning, especially the "meaning of life" or human nature, is Sartre's *Existentialism and Humanism*. On Sartre's view we tend to extend our concept of the human purpose for which manufactured articles are made to nonmanufactured items such as life, the world and man himself. And even though we may deny, in theory, any explicit reference to actual divine or cosmic purposes, our understanding of meaning, or the lack of it, is still, as Kant put it, "purposive" (*Zweckmässigkeit ohne Zweck*) [9] —the root of our thinking is still the anthropological concern with purposeful action, doing one thing "for the sake of" another. As Sartre puts it,

If one considers an article of manufacture—as, for example, a book or a paper-knife—one sees that it has been made by an artisan who had a conception of it ... and ... pre-existent technique of production which is a part of that conception and is, at bottom, a formula. Thus the paper-knife is at the same time an article producible in a certain manner and one which, on the other hand, serves a definite purpose, for one cannot suppose that a man would produce a paper-knife without knowing what it was for. Let us say, then, of the paper-knife that its essence—that is to say the sum of the formulae and the qualities which made its production and its definition possible—precedes its existence ... . Here, then, we are viewing the world from a technical standpoint ... . When we think of God as the creator, we are thinking of him ... as a super-natural artisan. Whatever doctrine we may be considering, ... we always imply that the will follows, more or

---

[9] Kant, Immanuel, *Critique of Judgment* (Bernard, trans.), New York: Hafner Publishing Co., 1951, pp. 25-29, 54-56.

less from the understanding or at least accompanies it, so that when God creates he knows precisely what he is creating. Thus, the conception of man in the mind of God is comparable to that of the paper-knife in the mind of the artisan: God makes man according to a procedure and a conception, following a definition and a formula. Thus each individual man is the realization of a certain conception which dwells in the divine understanding. In the philosophical atheisism of the eighteenth century, the notion of God is suppressed, but not ... the idea that essence ... is found in every man; which means that each man is a particular example of a universal conception, the conception of Man ... .[10]

Even where we no longer accept literally the existence of God, the idea of a divine plan lingers on in a quasi-intentional or purposive manner in the concept of a fixed and abiding human nature. As we will see, for both Plato and Leibniz, as well as Kant at least in regard to biology, a thing can be *fully* understood only in terms of the purpose for which it was designed (or seems to be designed).

Finally, despite the contemporary bias in favor of linguistic meaning as the primary sense, both Wittgenstein and Heidegger, who provide the conceptual foundations for most contemporary discussions of meaning, regard nonlinguistic meaning as basic—especially Wittgenstein's treatment of meaning in terms of a basic social pattern, or "form of life" [11] and Heidegger's related concern with the "horizon" of meaning as the ground of being-as, "that from which something is understandable as the thing it is," [12] which Heidegger understands as man's purposive "Being-in-the-world," a practical concern with things which puts them to use, a primary relationship to a world of things regarded as tools, or instruments (*das Zeug*) "for the sake of" writing, building, measurement, and so on.[13] Meaning for Heidegger, as for Wittgenstein, is ultimately the place of things in an interpreted "world," the world, in other words, as a system of relations as seen from an anthropological or social point of view. For Heidegger this means regarding everything as though designed to serve the needs of man, and hence, purposively. The forest is a part of our

[10] Sartre, Jean Paul, "Existentialism and Humanism," in: Morton White (ed.), *The Age of Reason*, A Mentor Book, 1955, pp. 122-124.
[11] Wittgenstein, Ludwig, *Remarks on the Logical Foundations of Mathematics* (G. E. M. Anscombe, trans.), Cambridge, Mass.: The M.I.T. Press, 1967, pp. 41-48, 110, 193-194.
[12] Heidegger, Martin, *Being and Time* (John McQuarrie and Edward Robinson, trans.), London: S.C.M. Press, 1962, pp. 192-193.
[13] *Ibid.*, p. 97.

world in the sense that it is for the sake of firewood, recreation, timber, providing a home for our ancestors, potential farmland, and so on.

Although linguistic meaning remains the most familiar and articulate concept of meaning, philosophers are coming to realize that linguistic meaning, and the possibility of linguistic meaning, can only be understood against such an anthropological background of nonlinguistic meaning. Indeed, many of these nonlinguistic senses have already been admitted "through the back door," as it were, as parts of *linguistic* meaning. What this amounts to is the gradual recognition that the meaning of words and sentences can only be understood by reference to human intentions, institutions, forms of social life, etc. But this is "linguistic" only by the wildest stretch of the imagination *and* the concept. To continue to speak of all this as "*linguistic* meaning" is simply clinging to a familiar framework which cannot be adequately enlarged to include the fullest dimensions of meaning. Certainly, it is only the loss of some sort of non-linguistic meaning which can explain the modern sense of meaninglessness. There is no difficulty seeing how one would go about locating the various senses of meaninglessness as the *lack* or *loss* of meaning in one or more of the nonlinguistic senses already discussed— meaninglessness, for example, as the lack of purpose or reason (the sense of absurdity), or the loss of a pattern or structure holding things together (the sense of things falling apart, of our being lost in a maze), the lack of any recognizable shape or form (the sense of strangeness, alienation), the loss of importance, savor, zest (the sense of being dead to life or love), the loss of a sense of the consequences of one's actions (the sense of impotence, hopelessness). This is precisely the kind of work already begun by Ilham Dilman in his thoughtful article, "Life and Meaning." [14]

Dilman distinguishes three basic senses of meaning, 1) the linguistic sense of dictionary meaning, 2) purpose and intention, and 3) the place of an action in the total pattern of a person's life. The meaninglessness of one's action, or of one's life, or of life generally, is directly related to the loss of meaning in this last sense—not simply the failure to know *what* an action or life means, in the way I know what "ja" or "procrastination" means, but the inability to see the interrelatedness of one's action, or of *any* of one's actions, in a total,

[14] Dilman, Ihlam, "Life and Meaning." *Philosophy*, vol. 40, 1965.

integrated system or pattern of life. When this happens we say our life has become meaningless, pointless, senseless or absurd.

As Dilman points out, people do ask, "Is my life meaningful?" as well as, "Is life (in general) meaningful?" though it is not immediately clear what sort of answer, if any, is wanted. Such a question may simply express one's inability to function in life or the fact that something has gone wrong with one's love or zest for life. But it may mean more than this, particularly as seen in the third-person question, "What makes *his* life meaningful?" This question may mean "What is it about his various activities which *add up* to something?" Or, it may suggest that the speaker *doesn't* find much in the other's life worth examining. Or, finally, it may mean that while the speaker concedes that such a life may add up to something for a certain type of person, he is not sure *what* type of person this is, or whether he can understand such a person. If I find his life meaningless, but he doesn't, I may feel that he is wasting his life, not enjoying it, not getting anything out of it, that what he does is futile and pointless. Or, I may find this *type* of life pointless, futile or empty. In the first case what I may be querrying is whether *he* really finds it meaningful, or whether he is not, perhaps, deluding himself. Dilman offers an example of two men disagreeing over the meaning and value of the one's marriage. The husband admits that the individual parts of the marriage, examined one by one, do not amount to much, but he defends the marriage by arguing that together they add up to something more.

It's like taking a lot of numbers that don't look alike and don't mean anything until you add them all together ... . There are the kids and the house ... . Of course, Kay and I do quarrel sometimes, but when you add it all together, all of it isn't as bad as the parts of it seem! [15]

Then, as Dilman points out, one may generalize this question by wondering what makes *anyone's* life meaningful, how in general meaningfulness is related to a person's life. With a nod to Austin, Dilman suggests that the meaning of a person's life can only be seen by contrast with what constitutes a *loss* of meaning. But the point is perhaps better understood in a phenomenological sense. The meaningfulness of life, like health, becomes noticeable only as we are losing it.

Dilman's main conclusion is that the meaning of one's life is to be

[15] *Ibid.*, p. 322.

understood in terms of what we described earlier as functional interdependency, the interrelatedness of parts within a total pattern. A person's life has multiple roots in the life of a larger social community. He derives, and must derive, his moral, intellectual and spiritual life from this human environment. When a man loses these roots his spirit dwindles and dries up. Compare D. H. Lawrence's analysis in "*A propos* of *Lady Chaterly's Lover*," where he describes modern man as "a great uprooted tree, with its roots in the air. We must plant ourselves again in the universe." [16] Or, at the other extreme from literature, consider Wittgenstein's view that what gives meaning to statements in mathematics or logic is the role they play in the broader life of a society.[17] Dilman draws out this parallel with Wittgenstein further. "Just as a person may speak and yet have nothing to say, so may a person do various things without finding much sense in what he does." [18] This means that it doesn't much matter to him whether he does this or that; what he does makes no sense to him, he feels himself simply going through the motions. "Having no purpose and interests, no heart to do anything, and having nothing to say—these go together." [19]

A person's actions can become meaningful only in and because or a social context. Hence, the sense of meaninglessness is typically symptomatic of social alienation and general cultural uprootedness. When his life loses meaning, he can derive nothing from culture, and without this he can no longer see himself in relation to others.

An extremely important point in Dilman's analysis to which we shall return is that there are certain perspectives or standpoints from which life invariably tends to look meaningless, of which Dilman mentions death and an "exaggerated vision of the selfishness of men." [20] As we will see, both these attitudes have the effect of flattening and neutralizing moral and other values, loosening their moral cohesiveness. The example Dilman considers is Tolstoy's story "The Death of Ivan Ilych." Tolstoy makes the reflections of the unphilosophic Ivan on the meaning of life believable by placing them within the perspective of Ivan's awareness of his impending death.

---

[16] Lawrence, D. H. "A propos of *Lady Chatterley's Lover*," in: *Phoenix II* (Warren Roberts and Harry Moore, ed.), New York: Viking Press, 1968, p. 510.

[17] Wittgenstein, *op. cit.*

[18] Dilman, *op. cit.*, p. 324.

[19] *Ibid.*, p. 325.

[20] *Ibid.*, p. 328.

It is entirely comprehensible that a plain man such as Ivan should realize on his death bed that "his life has come to nothing." How does Ivan come to this conclusion, and what does he mean?

He arrives at this judgment by a retrospective summing up of his life. Ivan has been a social climber, always eager to please. He adopts whatever attitude will advance him, and yet these attitudes are never really his. He begins to see that his life is strangely yet definitely alien to him. On the one hand it expresses only a part of him and on the other hand something false. He had within him, for example, the ability to love and care for others to which the actual indifference of his life was false and alien.

Why does Ivan only now, as he is dying, realize all of this? He now sees that he was in fact always on the verge of recognizing and denouncing his inadequate, inauthentic life, but always just managed in the end to avoid this painful self-knowledge, and to carry on the act, deceiving himself through bad faith. What then, in Ivan's estimation, makes his life meaningless? What, in other words, does he mean, exactly, when he says his life is meaningless? Summarizing, Dilman mentions three main elements; his self-alienation, his bad faith warding off guilt, fear and depression, and his inability to relate to others. And surely this, or something like it, is what young people have in mind when they condemn their middle class parents for leading empty, shallow and senseless lives? They see through, from their outside perspective, the self-alienation, the falseness, the hypocrisy, the emotional indifference, and disconnectedness from any seriously held values.

Granted, we have not yet given a coherent account of all this; so far we are only trying to itemize the various components, the pieces of the puzzle, as it were, in order to see the rich diversity of the contents before attempting to put the pieces together into some kind of intelligible order. It is not that there is nothing one understands, or can say, about meaninglessness; the difficulty is rather the opposite one of an overabundance of things we *do* understand and *are* able to ascribe to it. Meaninglessness, in its modern sense, can mean any of the following, or any combination thereof: being disconnected or uprooted; being impotent, or not in control of events; the moral or evaluative levelling of everything; the insignificance or alienation of man in a vast, nonhuman universe; the contingency of man; the hollowness or emptiness of life; the lack of a reason for living or a purpose to life; the failure of the world to answer to man's rationality; the fact that everything adds up to nothing, or very little; the pointlessness of life; the waste of one's life; mechanically going through the motions of life; loss of identity; the dog-eat-dog quality of life; the power of death to negate everything; the falseness, inauthenticity of one's life; indifference to others; a morally debased quality in things; having lost one's bearings and so on. The *experience* of meaninglessness can further be described as a feeling of inertia or ennui, as the alternation between feelings of suffocation and evanescence; as a loss of zest for life or interest in things; as a feeling for the strangeness or incomprehensibility of things; and so on. And, finally, without pretending to give a complete list, synonyms could be grouped under the following heads: absurd, insane; senseless, pointless, mechanical, disconnected; futile, empty, and illusory.

The difficulty lies in seeing how all this hangs together. As a first step in this direction, let us consider recent attempts to articulate the more important facets of the modern sense of meaninglessness, especially by those writers associated with Existentialism and the Theater of the Absurd, such as Sartre, Camus, Ionesco and Beckett.

There are two main existentialist senses of 'absurd': that the world is absurd because it is unreasonable, irrational, inexplicable, and that things are absurd because they have been stripped of the meanings we as human beings assign to them. Absurdity refers, then, either to a world without reason or to things without sense. We now turn to an examination of the first of these.

Absurdity, for Ionesco, is the final assault on an already crippled and dottering rationalism, the mainspring of Europe's philosophic, scientific and theological thought for over two thousand years though under increasing attack for the last two hundred. For Ionesco the view that everything, including man, occupies a rational and justifiable niche in a neatly ordered, thoroughly intelligible universe is not only false, but hypocritical and immoral. We must now see through this pretense as a deliberate construction of a false world, a constriction of the real world into a narrow straight-jacket. There is no reason for anything in the world, no final or immediate justification for man's existence, or for any of his actions. The world and human existence, seen from this point of view, is therefore senseless and absurd. As Martin Esslin points out, this is a perfectly proper use of the word "absurd," which originally meant "out of harmony" in a musical context and has now come to mean out of harmony with reason, hence, incongruous, unreasonable, or illogical.[21]

But for Ionesco this is not so much a philosophical position to be defined and clarified as a style of writing, a form of literature which strips the remaining familiar film of rationality from things to reveal the absurd reality beneath, inspiring him, as he says,

with a different logic and a different psychology, I should introduce contradiction where there is no contradiction, and no contradiction where there is what common sense usually calls contradiction ... . We'll get rid of the principle of identity and unity of character and let movement and dynamic psychology take its place.[22]

And, as Coe tries to show in his book, *Ionesco*, anti-rationalism in philosophy amounts to anti-realism in drama.

Realism in art ... is inseparable from rationalism; and rationalism itself, in its early stages, was inseparable from the growth of science ... . Whatever existed, existed therefore *rationally* and *necessarily*; and, in consequence, art, whose logic was assumed merely to be a by-product of the logic of science and mathematics, could have no higher ambition than to portray ... events and objects as they existed in the outside world ... . (But, when) it became evident ... that whatever laws the universe was governed by, it was by laws infinitely more subtle and complex than those of classical scientific rationalism, and consequently that 'realism,' far from portraying the 'only true and necessary' picture of existence, was in fact depicting a positive falsehood, the reaction was immediate: all that had ... been oppressed by the dictatorship of rationalism, came bursting to the surface, ... trying to elucidate the situation of the human spirit in a universe from which logic is absent, the 'necessary justification' of existence ... is similarly missing. In Ionesco, the fact of existence is neither logical nor justified. It is simply a fact; and existence without rational justification is, in the technical language of Existentialism, simply 'absurd' ... .[23]

As a result, much of Ionesco's work is designed to show how human logic can crumble. Logic is destroyed and nothing remains but an endless series of worthless, unrelated phenomena; as Coe puts it, "a world of infinite coincidence." [24] In such a world there is no such thing as familiarity or coherent experience or the possibility of reasonable explanation, as Kant saw long ago and from which he

[21] Esslin, Martin, *The Theatre of the Absurd*, Harmondsworth, England: Penguin Books, Ltd., 1968, p. 23.

[22] Ionesco, Eugene in Coe, Richard N., *Ionesco*, London: Oliver and Boyd, Ltd., 1961, p. 17.

[23] Coe, *Ibid.*, pp. 23-25.

[24] *Ibid.*, p. 27.

sought to defend us. Everything is at once equally amazing and equally banal. As Ionesco says, "everything is brought down to the same level, everything is drowned in the general improbability and unlikelihood of the universe itself." [25] Laws of space, time, causality and physical objects, as well as the unity of personality, are abandoned; there is no continuity from one moment to the next, from one experience to the next.

As a result of this universal coincidence, words become disassociated from feelings, thoughts, things and projects, and language becomes a meaningless stuffing to fill the gap of meaninglessness. In the absence of an intelligible world of recognizable objects and in the absence of a stable personality, words become substitutes for things, feelings, thoughts, relationships, and speech becomes debased, shorn of meaning. Detached from life and experience, words begin to take on a menacing life of their own. "In the absence of meaning, the words themselves take absolute control, and drive their unfortunate victim whithersoever their blind and dangerous energies may so direct." [26] In short, the world

appears illusory and fictitious, where human behaviour reveals its absurdity, and all history its absolute uselessness; all reality, all language seems to become disjointed, to fall apart, to empty itself of meaning, so that, since all is devoid of importance, what else can one do but laugh at it? [27]

The chief psychological effect of absurdity, in Ionesco, is an alternating sense of lightness and heavyness, an alternation between the emptiness of a world devoid of meaning and the suffocating, crushing weight of a world of mere things devoid of meaning, simply filling up space, crowding us out. On the one hand, "we seem to see through everything in a universe without space, made up only of light and colour; all our existence, all the history of the world becomes at this moment useless, senseless, impossible ... ." [28] And on the other hand, as in Sartre's description of nausea, we are filled with an oppressive sense of the sheer otherness of inanimate objects, in which "matter fills everything, takes up all space, annihilates all liberty under its weight; the horizon shrinks and the world becomes a stifling dungeon. Speech crumbles, but in another way ... words,

---

[25] Ionesco, *L'Invraisemblable*, in: Coe, *op. cit.*, p. 28.

[26] Coe, *op. cit.*, p. 43.

[27] Ionesco, Eugene, "Point of Departure" (L. C. Pronko, trans.), *Theatre Arts*, vol. 42, no. 6, 1958, p. 17.

[28] *Ibid.*

obviously devoid of magic, are replaced by accessories, by objects
.... " 29

Camus also describes absurdity as the profound absence of reason
—no reason to live, no reason for doing, no reason for anything.
In *The Myth of Sisyphus* Camus carries this idea to its logical extreme,
bringing to a fine point the central question of meaninglessness:
"does the lack of any reason for living logically demand or morally
sanction suicide?" Can one find "within the limits of nihilism ... the
means to proceed beyond nihilism?" [30] Camus' answer, of course,
is 'yes,' but we are concerned now with Camus' statement of the
problem rather than his answer to it. The main feature of absurdity
is its irrationality.

You continue making the gestures commanded by existence for many
reasons, the first of which is habit. Dying voluntarily implies that you have
recognized, even instinctively, the ridiculous character of that habit, the
absence of any profound reason for living, the insane character of that
daily agitation, and the uselessness of suffering.[31]

In such a world, nothing is explainable, intelligible, accountable;
hence nothing is familiar, everything is strange and alien.

A world that can be explained even with bad reasons is a familiar world.
But, on the other hand, in a universe suddenly divested of illusions and
lights, man feels an alien, a stranger .... This divorce between man and
his life, the actor and his setting, is properly called the feeling of absurdity.[32]

Absurdity is the hopeless contradiction of man's desire for rationality
and the inherently irrational nature of the universe.

Of particular interest is Camus' analysis of the stages by which
absurdity enters one's experience. The first stage is the awareness
that the connections holding things together into a coherent world
are breaking up, that things are falling apart,

That odd state of the soul in which the void becomes eloquent, in which
the chain of daily gestures is broken, in which the heart vainly seeks the
link that will connect it again, then it is as it were the first signs of absurdity.[33]

---

[29] *Ibid.*
[30] Camus, Albert, *The Myth of Sisyphus* (Justin O'Brien, trans.), New York:
Vintage Books, 1960, p. v.
[31] *Ibid.*, p. 5.
[32] *Ibid.*
[33] *Ibid.*, p. 10.

0142771

83091

Next one sees oneself inextricably linked with the passage of time
travelling through an empty landscape toward death. And finally,
one reaches that state which Sartre describes as nausea, the sense
of the complete otherness of inanimate, nonhuman things. Devoid
of the technological, scientific, commercial and romantic meanings
we have projected on to the world, things become *mere* things,
a hateful reality utterly distinct from human meanings.

A step lower and strangeness creeps in: perceiving that the world is 'dense,'
sensing to what degree a stone is foreign and irreducible to us, with what
intensity nature or a landscape can negate us. At the heart of all beauty
lies something inhuman, and these hills, the softness of the sky, ... at this
very minute lose the illusory meaning with which we had clothed them ... .[34]

The absurd world is alien because it is inhuman and it is inhuman
because it is devoid of human reasons, explanations, and concepts.

The mind's deepest desire ... is an insistance upon familiarity, an appetite
for clarity. Understanding the world for a man is reducing it to the human,
stamping it with his seal ... . The mind that aims to understand reality
can consider itself satisfied only by reducing it to terms of thought.[35]

Without this the world and man's life is alien, senseless and absurd.

Earlier we mentioned Dilman's position that certain points of view
appear inevitably to reveal meaninglessness. One such point of view
is the absolutist stance of the man who views the world *sub specie
aeternatatis*, from the standpoint of "what will it matter 5000 years
from now." From the aspect of eternity everything seems contingent,
futile, pointless and scarcely worth the effort. If it's not going to
make a difference 5000 years from now, or in the scope of things,
then does it really matter now? This type of perspective reveals
meaninglessness as the insignificance of man and the futility of his
action when seen against the backdrop of infinite space and time.

Pascal, who may still be considered a philosophical contemporary,
has probably given the best statement of this view of absurdity.

When I consider the tiny span of my life, which is swallowed up in the
eternity which precedes and follows it, when I consider the tiny space that
I occupy and can even see, lost as I am in the infinite immensity of Space
which I know nothing about and which knows nothing about me, I am
terrified and marvel to find myself here rather than there, for there is no

---

[34] *Ibid.*, p. 11.
[35] *Ibid.*, p. 13.

reason at all why here rather than there or why now rather than then. Who put me there? By whose command and under whose direction were this time and this place destined for me? [36]

This is generally a religiously motivated standpoint, an either/or stance between an absolutely eternal and transcendent source of meaning and a pathetic and utterly pointless existence. Later we will challenge this attitude, but now we simply want to understand it as a type and source of meaninglessness.

In his essay on Kafka, Ionesco says:

Absurd is that which is devoid of purposes ... . Cut off from his religious, metaphysical, and transcendental roots, man is lost; all his actions become senseless, absurd, useless.[37]

This indicates a more theoretical or metaphysical approach to meaninglessness, a philosophical reflection which may *lead* to a *feeling* of meaninglessness but which is not quite *identical* with it. It's as though we quite literally used to have an absolutely final answer to the question, "what is the meaning of life?" an answer, as we saw in Sartre, based on the analogy between man's purposeful relation to manufactured goods and God's relation to man. The reason for man's existence is tied to God's purposes and plans for man, and if we can no longer believe in God, then this answer becomes false, or at least empty and useless.

Another writer whose view of the absurd springs from this absolutist point of view is Adamov. To Adamov the world *must* have some hidden transcendent meaning which guarantees the significance of the world as a whole and everything in it. When we lose sight of this transcendent meaning or purpose, we are completely lost, our lives thoroughly wasted and futile. In "Pain, 1938" he wrote, "at the origin of myself there is mutilation, separation," [38] a separation from a sense of unity with the sacred, absolute purpose and meaning of the world.

From whatever point he starts, whatever path he follows, modern man comes to the same conclusion: behind its visible appearances, life hides a meaning that is eternally inaccessible to penetration by the spirit that

---

[36] Pascal, Blaise, *Thoughts* (W. F. Trotter, trans.), in: *The Harvard Classics*, vol. 48, New York: P. F. Collier and Son, Co., 1910, p. 78.

[37] Ionesco, in: Esslin, *op. cit.*, p. 23.

[38] Adamov, Arthur, "The Endless Humiliation" (Richard Howard, trans.), *Evergreen Review*, vol. 2, no. 8, 1959, p. 66.

seeks for its discovery, caught in the dilemma of being aware that it is impossible to find it, and yet also impossible to renounce the hopeless quest.[39]

And, of course, this presupposes that, like the pen-knife, the world *has* a meaning, that behind the world of experience there is something, however ellusive, which gives it meaning. Without the key to this hidden meaning we are like the characters in *Le Ping-Pong*, wasting our lives in the futile pursuit of phantoms. As Esslin points out, for Adamov, "all human endeavor comes down to the same futility —a senile whittling away of the remaining time before death reduces everything to final absurdity." [40]

Meaninglessness from the absolutist standpoint turns on a very special view of time which is probably best expressed in Beckett. For Beckett the span of time (as seen from the standpoint of eternity) collapses, levelling and shortening everything. "The more things change, the more they are the same" expresses the central paradox of time in practically all of Beckett's writing. The characters in Beckett's plays are usually seen aimlessly waiting, passing time, idling away the hours, under a very fragile illusion of purposeful anticipation and expectation.

In *Waiting for Godot* Estragon and Vladimir are waiting for something to happen, but since, in Beckett's view, nothing real ever does happen, change is an illusion and any human activity, self-defeating and pointless. Hence, the more things change, the more they are the same. This vision of human activity arises from a detached, absolute point of view, like standing back, watching ants scurrying back and forth, just as they have always done for thousands, millions of years, never stopping but never really getting anywhere. Since nothing important or significant is really happening, or getting accomplished, temporal extension is unreal, and time ironically shrinks. Time without the possibility of meaningful, purposeful action contracts, shortening everything in its path; there is no more significance to the space of 80 years than to 80 seconds. Hence the sense of a man stretching out his life with activity and accomplishment is an illusion; he is dead (or as good as dead) as soon as he is born. As Pozzo says,

Have you not done tormenting me with your accursed time? ... One day, is that not enough for you, one day like any other day he went dumb,

---

[39] *Ibid.*
[40] Esslin, *op. cit.*, p. 112.

one day I went blind, one day we'll go deaf, one day we were born, one day we'll die, the same day, same second ... . They gave birth astride of a grave, the light gleams an instant, then it's night once more.[41]

Ultimately it is death, of course, which, on this view, flattens and shortens life, swallowing up any would-be purposeful "end" of life and action in the final temporal "end" of each man's life. Death, like the infinity or eternity of time, not only annihilates man, but retrospectively annihilates the point of any human action, robbing it of reason and purpose. If I look at my own projects or national and international projects from the point of view of their eventual and inevitable demise, I can no longer attach any point or purpose, and hence reason, to these activities. To act meaningfully is to act purposely, doing one thing for the sake of another. This presupposes the possibility of accomplishing certain ends. But it is death, when viewed from this absolutist standpoint, which seems to rob any possible action of its accomplishment. In the short run things may appear to be worthwhile, but not in the long run, that is, not from the standpoint of eternity. If I plan a career, or the education of my children, or work toward a system of international security, then, however successful I am in the short run, all of this will be negated in the long run by the death of myself and my children and the eventual cosmic death of our planet. And, from this Olympian retrospective point of view, this not only *will be* negated, but *is now*, in reality, that is, *sub specie aeternitatis*. From this point of view, there is no distinction, except in illusion, between the accomplishment of Ozymandias as viewed by Ozymandias himself and as seen by the narrator in Shelley's poem. Death annihilates all, including the extendedness of time itself.

Even in the short run, according to Sartre and Heidegger, negation and nothingness invade purposeful human action. Planning involves selecting one of several, not actually existing, goals. This presupposes an awareness of negation both in the sense of choosing something which is not now existing and in the sense of eliminating alternative possibilities, deciding that they should not exist.

Another important feature of absurdity which we've already mentioned is man's alienation both from himself and from the outside world. In Genet this appears as the helpless, lonely solitude of a man trapped in a maze of mirrors which reflect nothing but distorted

---

[41] Beckett, Samuel, *Waiting for Godot*, London: Faber and Faber, 1959, p. 89.

projections of his own disconnected self. This image conveys both the nothingness of man's internal self and that of the external world. Cut off from external reality we have no fixed point of reference from which to judge objectively ourselves and reality. Each glimpse of myself or my world is built on a sliding and inexhaustible series of lies—lies based on lies, fantasies fed by fantasies, illusions supported by further illusions. The meaning we assign to ourselves and to the world is only a flickering projection of shifting facets of ourself, itself a projection and hence an illusion. Locked within this hopeless situation one can only reach out to intangible and contradictory excretions of oneself; hence the desperate loneliness and solitude in Genet's vision of absurdity.

So much for the first sense of absurdity in the Existentialist litera-ture, the lack of reason in the world. We turn now to the second major sense, that of things stripped of humanly assigned meanings. If we understand the first, as I think we can, as the absence of meaning either in the sense of the interrelatedness of things within a system or the purposeful reason for something, then we may understand the second primarily as the absence of being-as. According to this interpretation, meanings are human values with which we invest things which are in themselves meaninglessness. Thus, when these essentially human meanings are stripped from things, we are brought face to face with the brute, alien, inhuman aspect of mere things choking and crowding us out. But just because these things are without significance, they are in that sense nothing and consequently ethereal, fleeting and unreal. Hence, the alternating sense of oppressive heaviness and evanescent lightness so often described by Existentialist writers, that surrealist tension between the all-too-real and the dreamlike quality of things which Ionesco expresses so well.

Two fundamental states of consciousness are at the root of all my plays ... those of evanescence on the one hand, and heaviness on the other; of emptiness and of an over-abundance of presence; of the real transparancy of the world, and of its opaqueness; of light, and of heavy shadows.[42]

This sense of absurdity is probably best described by Sartre, not so much in *Being and Nothingness*, where this is expressed philosophically in terms of his distinction between being-in-itself (brute things without human meanings) and being-for-itself (human reason-giving and meaning-projection), but psychologically in the novels, especially

[42] Ionesco, "Point of Departure," *op. cit.*

Nausea. The experience Sartre calls nausea is a sense of things as totally other, encroaching on us, threatening us simply because they are not like us. This is a view of reality stripped of man's projected meanings, "being" without meaning, hemming us in, stifling us.

Because inanimate objects are alien, they are vaguely repulsive.

Objects should not *touch* because they are not alive. You use them, put them back in place, you live among them; they are useful, nothing more. But they touch me; it is unbearable.[43]

Unlike Genet, the feeling of nausea is basically outer-directed, a sense of being trapped within a world of dead, inhuman things from which there is no escape, the absence of an abode we could properly call home. "The Nausea is not inside me; I feel it *out there* in the wall, in the suspenders, everywhere around me ... . I am the one who is within it." [44] To say that things are inhuman is not just to say that they are not human beings, but that humanly projected meanings will no longer attach to them.

I murmer: 'It's a seat,' a little like an exorcism. But the words stay on my lips: it refuses to go and put itself on the thing. It stays what it is ... . Things are divorced from their names. They are there, grotesque, headstrong, gigantic and it seems ridiculous to call them seats or say anything at all about them; I am in the midst of things, nameless things. Alone without words, defenceless, they surround me ... .[45]

Here the brute, bullying otherness of things weighs in upon us with the suffocating heaviness described by Ionesco. But the next moment we experience the alternative lightness, emptiness of things. Shorn of meaning they exist, are just there, heavily and oppressively; but shorn of meaning they are also nothing. *What* are these things (i.e., what do we *call* them, what *meaning* do we attach to them)? Nothing. Hence, they *are*, in this sense, nothing; they have existence in the technical sense of reality without meaning, but they have no being-as, no being or essence. They are *there*, but they don't exist *for us*. Hence, their overt heaviness dissolves into an empty, hollow unreality.

Today they fixed nothing at all: it seemed that their very existence was subject to doubt, that they had the greatest difficulty in passing from one

[43] Sartre, Jean Paul, *Nausea* (Lloyd Alexander, trans.), Norfolk, Conn.: New Directions Books, 1959, p. 19.
[44] *Ibid.* p. 31.
[45] *Ibid.*, p. 169.

instant to the next. I held the book I was reading tightly in my hand; but the most violent sensations went dead. Nothing seemed true; I felt surrounded by cardboard scenery.[46]

Since meaning will no longer attach to these things, neither will explanation. Like Camus, Sartre's view of reality without meaning is the image of a surd (hence absurd), irreducible and recalcitrant element.

Absurd, irreducible; nothing ... could explain it ... the world of explanation and reasons is not the world of existence. A circle is not absurd, it is clearly explained ... . But neither does a circle exist. This root, on the other hand, existed in such a way that I could not explain it. Knotty, inert, nameless ... . In vain to repeat; 'this is a root'—it didn't work any more. I saw clearly that you could not pass from its function as a root, as a breathing pump, *to that*, to this hard and compact skin of a sea lion, to this oily, callous, headstrong look.[47]

We can't describe or explain or understand it; as far as we are concerned it is *just there*. "The essential thing is contingency. I mean that one cannot define existence as necessary, to exist is simply to *be there*." [48]

For Sartre the emotional response to this is two-fold; a repugnance at this proliferation of alien things choking and crowding us, and a sense of being unwanted, not at home in such a world.

I sank down on the bench, stupefied, stunned by this profusion of beings without origin: everywhere blossoming, hatching out, ... It was repugnant.[49]

We were a heap of living creatures, irritated, embarrassed at ourselves, we hadn't the slightest reason to be there, none of us, each one, confused, vaguely alarmed, felt in the way in relation to the others. *In the way*.[50]

But the main factor in Sartre's account of this alien reality is the separation of being from meaning; existence for Sartre is being without being-as, or as he prefers to put, existence without essence. "I was not surprised, I knew it was the World, the naked World suddenly revealing itself, and I choked with rage at this gross, absurd being." [51]

---

[46] *Ibid.*, p. 106.
[47] *Ibid.*, p. 174.
[48] *Ibid.*, p. 176.
[49] *Ibid.*, pp. 178-179.
[50] *Ibid.*, p. 172.
[51] *Ibid.*, p. 180.

This is perhaps the most philosophically prominent concept of meaninglessness, especially as it has been developed by writers like Wild and Blackman.

The intelligible world constructed by personal existence, in which man feels safe and at home, the world of meanings, is nihilated and he is plunged back into the sheer 'is-ness' of what is … . This is an experience of brute existence denuded of meanings … . It uncovers the marvellousness of pure 'is-ness,' contingency, which reason covers up, and is therefore a revelation of Being.[52]

Wild regards meaninglessness as the clash between being and meaning, the awareness of being as *lacking* meaning. But if one is standpoint-bound, as we agreed earlier, *can* one be aware of being without meaning, without interpretation? This is where Wild professes to disagree with Heidegger who regards being as coextensive with meaning. Even though the reality we find in our "world" is an interpreted reality ("being" merged with meaning), such a world is only possible, on Wild's view, against the backdrop of a "world-horizon" which includes both interpreted items and items which lack but demand interpretation, as well as items for which there are conflicting and competing interpretations. In this broader sense, the world includes multiple versions and potential versions, which interpreted being does not. Things in the world can also have *degrees* of meaning.

This is an important point. Surely, the world I am aware of includes items *to be* clarified, things which *require* or *call for* interpretation; perhaps we understand them in *some* way but only minimally. Also, and this too is important, interpreted reality, being-as, is recognized as finite and incomplete. Only if this were the case would it be possible to press, as we do, for a *fuller* grasp, a *deeper* understanding of some event or person, or to try to discover, as we do, what really happened regarding some historical event, such as John Kennedy's assassination. It is for this reason that Wild distinguishes "Being₁," the thing in itself, from "Being₂," the revealed meaning of X, as the two poles of experienced reality.

Part of Wild's justification for this position is that it accords with

[52] Blackman, H. J., *Six Existentialist Thinkers*, New York: Harper, 1952, p. 104.

our experience of absurdity, the "clashing dissonance between being and meaning that has been widely experienced in our time." [53]

Being is not necessarily joined with meaning as the major stream of Western thought, and also Heidegger, have supposed. Contrary to these teachings they may fall apart, and they may have fallen apart in the world of our time.[54]

When meaning vanishes, being (Being) remains, the "enormous plethora of senseless beings" [55] (Coleridge's "mass of little things") which Sartre describes as the feeling of nausea. Thus, the opposite of meaning is not nothingness, as Heidegger and Sartre contend, but meaninglessness, i.e., meaningless *being*. The opposite of nothingness is being, but this is precisely what is revealed when meaning is stripped away.

Part of the dispute between Wild and Heidegger is based on misunderstanding. The point is, *do* we have an experience of being without meaning? Well, in one sense, we do, and this is what Wild stresses, but in another sense, we do not, and this is Heidegger's point. To the extent that I recognize that my knowledge of X is incomplete I have some concept of X itself, but, *ex hypothesi*, I *don't* have an experience of this thing in itself, and in that sense it is *not* part of the world of my experience. This accords with ordinary speech. When I say I want to know what X is really like it is understood that I am intellectually pushing toward something which I know is there but don't fully comprehend. The beauty of Wild's account is that he allows a place for this revelation of the thing itself in our everyday experience. But, on the other hand, I never *fully* comprehend X; that is, I never actually completely succeed in grasping the thing itself, and this is where Heidegger scores a point—in this sense we *are* standpoint-bound. I know the *thing itself* to the extent that I have partial information about X. I have some regulative concept of the thing *in* itself in the empty hypothetical sense that I know that my partial interpretation is only an interpretation *of* X and not X itself and in *that* sense the thing in itself is an operational but unfulfilled concept in my world; but I do *not* have any understanding of X *apart* from any partial interpretations *of* X (and in *that* sense the

---

[53] Wild, John, "Being, Meaning and the World", *Review of Metaphysics*, vol. 18, 1964, p. 427.
[54] *Ibid.*
[55] *Ibid.*, p. 426.

thing in itself does not and cannot enter my experience). Even the experience of nausea is the experience *that* things transcend the meanings we impose on them, *not* the experience of *what* this transcendent thing *is*, for what could this be for us but another *meaning* which, *ex hypothesi*, this brute thing does *not* have. Reality is like the carrot dangled before the donkey; it leads us on but we never actually eat it. The thing itself (being minus meaning) *does* function in our experience, and for this insight we are grateful to Wild, but only in the manner Kant ascribed to regulative concepts, that is, there is never any instantiation of the concept the-thing-itself, and for this our debt goes to Heidegger.

So, when Heidegger speaks of nothingness he does not mean the mere absence of existing things; he means the absence of *meaning in* existing things. This is why we speak of the nothingness *of things*; nothingness is a characteristic, albeit a negative characteristic, of things which exist. Later we will see that this is part of what the Buddhists mean when they speak of the emptiness of things—not the absence of anything in the world, which is unthinkable, but the absence in reality of the human meanings we project on the world.

But we are getting ahead of ourselves. Unavoidably, our descriptive inventory of different senses of meaning and meaninglessness has begun to suggest the outlines of a more simplified explanatory model. Different senses of meaning are already beginning to coalesce around certain central foci which can be summarized as follows.

1) Intention
    a) having good intentions (He meant well.)
    b) action intended (Do you mean to go now?)
    c) person or thing intended (Did you mean Jonathan?)
    d) purpose for which something is designed (It was meant to be a footstool.)

2) Connections between things
    a) practical consequences of an action (This means he will quit.)
    b) importance of X to someone, or the emotion aroused by X (Money means little to me.)
    c) association between things (Bees mean honey.)
    d) natural connections between things (Dark clouds mean rain.)
    e) the place of X in a system, especially the intended place of X in a social system (Paying the bride-price means that the two families whose children they want married have agreed on the

value representing the young man's ability to support his wife, his esteem for the girl's family, etc. etc.)

3) Being-as (For these people, being a chair means something to sit on while visiting, eating, reading—a piece of furniture.)

4) Identity or translation meaning
   a) linguistic ("Ja" means "yes".)
   b) dreams, etc. (The house means the womb. The Ace of Spades means death.)

Important links between these major strands of meaning are also beginning to emerge, which we will explore more fully in the next chapter.

And, finally, this pattern is already imposing itself on our attempt to itemize various senses of meaninglessness of which the most important are as follows:

1) lack of purpose or intention
   a) the absurd irrationality of things
   b) the evaluative levelling of things through death and the infinity of time
   c) the pointless futility of life

2) lack of connection between things
   a) being disconnected, uprooted
   b) being lost
   c) the clash of reason and reality

3) loss of a sense of being-as
   a) the repugnant otherness of mere things devoid of meaning
   b) feeling unwanted, not at home in an alien world
   c) estranged from things, alone

CHAPTER 2

THE UNITY OF MEANING

We must now try to reduce this diversity of meaning to some intelligible order. We have already distinguished four main senses of meaning:

1) the place of X in a system
2) human intention
3) linguistic or symbolic (identity or translation) meaning
4) being-as

Some suggestions about the relationships between these main senses have also been made. Linguistic meaning, for example, is obviously related to the speaker's intention. "What does that (statement) mean" often means "What did *he* mean?" in the sense of "What was his purpose, or motive in saying that?" Like most things conventional, what is originally an intention eventually becomes in effect a social fact. We often distinguish the meaning intended by the speaker from the conventional meaning of the words themselves. But, of course, the latter is also the meaning "intended" by the speaker's language-group. Once the convention is well established, the meaning tends to get transferred in the minds of the language-users to the words themselves. But this should not be allowed to obscure the basic fact that the meaning of any form of words is the meaning the speakers mean them to have. As the intention becomes public rather than private it begins to lose the look of an intention, but the intention is still there in the background in the *basic* intentional structure of speech.

Linguistic meaning is also, though less clearly, related to being-as in the sense that linguistic meaning presupposes the recognition of things as being of a certain kind. In order to meaningfully refer to something as a chair, I must be able to *see* it as a chair; that is, I must be able to recognize it as the sort of thing one sits in, reads in, and so on. And linguistic meaning is also joined to the interrelatedness of things in a system, both in the narrow sense of contextual meaning and in the broader sense of the form of life or anthropological background discussed earlier.

Being-as is related both to the systematic togetherness of things and to intention in that we often recognize a thing as the kind of thing it is by seeing its place in a larger system of things or as intended by someone. I understand a man's running for a bus by seeing its relation to the man's intention to catch the bus. I also understand it in terms of a whole interrelated pattern of social behavior—people having jobs, the importance of being punctual, living away from one's place of work, the nature of public transport not to wait for any particular person but to run according to schedule, and so on.

The place of X in a system of things is related to being-as in the sense that being-as is both its starting point and its end-product. What gets related in the system, the terms of the relation, are not blank ciphers, but recognizable units, and once we see the relation of parts fitting into some kind of whole, then the system as a whole takes on an implicit air of familiarity. As we pointed out earlier, taking note of these systematic relationships is a more self-conscious, explicit form of the everyday familiarity with the system, the sense of being at home within it, or at least of *not* being *not* at home in it. The systematic interrelatedness of things is also linked rather importantly with intention, for it usually turns out that the system or pattern is composed of many purposive or intentional (or quasi-intentional) relations. The man is running in order to catch the bus, the bus is going on ahead in order to keep to schedule, the man wants to catch the bus in order to get to work on time, in order to perform his work properly, keep his job, avoid waiting for another bus, and so on. I recognize my book case as something for the purpose of holding books, for the sake of locating them, for the sake of reading them, for the sake of research, for the sake of truth, prestige, a better job, and so on, and so on.

The meaning of particular sorts of things may spread over all four of these basic senses, shifting somewhat in meaning in each case. The meaning of language, as we have seen, can be either translation meaning, intention, or in the case of being-as, the recognizable familiarity of words themselves. A particular word sounds right for that object (or occasionally, as children discover, words suddenly

begin to sound strange); words sometimes seem to be almost inter-
changeable with the things they stand for. Because they are recognizable in their own right words can become the surrogate for
thoughts and things acquiring a life of their own, and, as Ionesco
and Sterne saw, get between us and the world they are intended to
reveal.

Dream meaning can be understood either as translation meaning,
contextual meaning or quasi-intentional meaning. That is, when we
ask what the red deer in the dream means, we may be asking for a
straightforward answer such as "ambition," "fear," "your mother,"
etc., or we may be inquiring into its relation with other items in the
dream, or we may expect an answer in terms of a quasi-intentional
communication from the subconscious.

Interestingly, "the meaning of life" also falls into all four of these
categories with a slightly different result in each case. We have
emphasized the meaning of life as the interrelatedness of one's
actions in a total integrated pattern having a place in the larger life
of the community. There is also the meaning of life as something
which has taken on a recognizable shape, or at least negatively,
the loss of which shape is experienced as meaninglessness. And there
is also the meaning of life in the sense of the purpose for one's life
or for mankind as a whole which we found in Sartre, and this can
lead to a sense of the meaning of life like that of translation meaning
in which one expects the same kind of answer to the question "what
is the meaning of life?" as to the question "what does '*ja*' mean?"

To carry our examination further, let us try to analyze the con-
ditional relationship between these main senses of meaning transcendentally, arranging the four, in other words, in a hierarchy of
presuppositional priority. The correct order, I suggest, is as follows:

1) linguistic or symbolic meaning
2) being-as
3) systematic interrelatedness
4) purpose and intention

Linguistic meaning presupposes being-as; being-as presupposes the
systematic interrelatedness of things; and this presupposes purpose
and intention. Knowing what the word "table" means presupposes
the ability to see that *as* a table, but this depends on an understanding
of the place that thing occupies in a system of socially intelligible
relations (i.e., seeing it as something to write on, eat off of, put

flowers on, etc.). And this type of understanding would be impossible without our ability to assign purposeful or intentional relationships to things (tables designed for the purpose of, intended to be used as this or that, etc.).

This brings out the priority of nonlinguistic meaning which is further supported by etymology. The first reference to the meaning of words is around 1000 A.D., following two centuries of non-linguistic meaning in the sense of saying and intending. Even then, linguistic meaning was used almost interchangeably with the non-linguistic sense of the speaker's intention, or as an extension of the latter in the sense that a word had the meaning which the speaker intended it to have. This is like referring to "what the book says" as an elliptical way of describing what the *author* says *in* the book. Linguistic meaning, in other words, in its early stages, appears to have been used in the elliptical sense of what the *speaker* means. Not until the 17th century is meaning tied in one of its uses to language in any nonelliptical way. With both "meaning" and "mean" there is first the sense of *having* an intention, and then of *that which* is intended, and only finally as a feature of that which is used to *convey* or *express* the intention.

"Meaningful," "meaningless," and "meaninglessness" occur much later, coming into widespread usage about the time of the Romantic concern with meaning, i.e., around 1795-1849. In fact, one can find three distinct phases in the etymological history of "meaning." First, from 1000-1590, there is the nonthematic use of having and stating intention (and later of that which is intended or which expresses what is intended). This is followed in the 17th century by the theoretical, self-conscious epistemological and psychological concern, e.g., of Locke, with linguistic meaning, and ending with the early 19th century equally self-conscious concern of Romantics like Lamb, Coleridge, and Ruskin with the loss of meaning and of securing a threatened meaning, now seen explicitly as something which can be, or has been, lost.

Even the natural and associative relation between things, so dear to semanticists like Richards, can only be understood in terms of purpose and intention (clouds pointing to rain, bees for the sake of honey). Without this at least quasi-intentional connection, natural and associative links between things would not count as a kind of meaning. Buzzing means bees, but bees don't mean buzzing (bees mean *honey*). Why not? If there is a natural connection between buzzing and bees, then equally there should be a natural connection between bees and buzzing. The reason would seem to be that buzzing means bees in the sense that buzzing *points to*, leads to or indicates bees and this presupposes the idea of intention which is not true of the relation of bees to buzzing. Similarly, dark clouds mean rain, but not the other way round. The point is more obvious, of course, in the case of meaning as the practical consequences of an action, which always involves an element of at least quasi-intention ("This means he'll quit." "Passage of this bill will mean the end of second-class citizenship.") This is why we blame a person for the consequences of his action; insofar as these may be foreseen they are intended in the action, or at least the burden of proof is on the agent to show that they are not. Richards, then, has latched on to a relatively minor sense which his positivist abhorence of the intentional side of meaning is unable to support. Because of the positivist axe he has to grind he avoids intentional meaning in favor of objective entities and relations between them, allowing cognition only a raw emotion directed toward these objects; but without intention Richards can't make sense even of this natural and associative meaning, much less the other forms of meaning which rely more heavily on intention.

Thus, the logical root of meaning can be traced to the sense of purpose and a system of purposeful relations. When people speak of the meaningfulness of things, they are usually talking either about (a) the purposive way things seem to hang together or (b) the purpose which this system has as a whole. Correspondingly, meaninglessness can mean either (a) the breakdown of this system or (b) the realization that the purpose for the system as a whole is a human projection having no foundation in reality. The second sense (b) indicates a more theoretical reflection of a predominantly metaphysical or religious nature, while the first (a) is primarily a psychological response. Nonetheless, the two are closely related, as suggested by our proposed scheme of transcendental relations between the major senses of meaning—though interestingly, the order of *meaningless* relationships will be the exact reverse of the *meaning* relationships. Meaninglessness as the loss of purpose and intention leads to meaninglessness as the loss of any systematic interrelatedness, leading to meaninglessness as the loss of linguistic meaning. If we ask, in a mood of metaphysical or religious reflection, what is the ultimate purpose of life or the world as a whole, then, assuming we can find no answer, we may be overcome by the psychological experience that the world is falling apart. We are then no longer able to relate one thing to another, nor ourselves to anything in a system or pattern of meanings. As a result things lose their familiar, recognizable shape and take on a disturbing strangeness. When this happens words cease to convey meaning or to disclose a meaningful world and become themselves disconnected, meaningless "things."

We will discuss this progressive dissolution of meaning more fully in Chapter 3; now we are simply noting that the philosophical reflection on the lack of any purpose for the world as a whole can lead to the psychological experience of the world-system falling apart, while the psychological experience of the collapse of a world is often accompanied either by the rationale that life has no purpose or the attempt to establish that there *is* some transcendent, ultimate purpose.

Adamov's play *L'Invasion* is a brilliant parable of the hopeless quest for the transcendent meaning or purpose which will make sense of and unify a mass of otherwise unintelligible, unrelated phenomena. Agnes is left with a mass of posthumous papers which she tries to decipher and put into some intelligible order; but she can't find the code, and the action of the play expresses that frenetic activity which really accomplishes nothing. Here meaning stands for harmony, the purposive fitting together of parts within a whole. But for Adamov this is only possible by means of a key or code, that is, meaning in the sense of a transcendent purpose or design for the system as a whole. Nothing short of this will show us how the pieces of the puzzle fit together. In other words, for Adamov, meaning in sense 3 depends entirely on meaning in sense 4.[1]

I have already mentioned Esslin's observation that "absurd" originally meant musically out of harmony, coming gradually to mean out of harmony in a more general way. From Dilman and Rankin we have got some idea of meaning in the sense of a purposeful pattern, while our discussion of Sartre and Camus has focused on meaning as the purpose which this behavioral pattern does or does not have as a whole. As Kant suggests, even when we ask for the meaning of a work of art or a part thereof, it is usually in the sense either of the artist's intention or the quasi-intention expressed in the work of art, or, what comes to much the same thing, the purposively-described relationships within the painting. "What does that mean?"

[1] Adamov, Arthur, *L'Invasion*, in: *Théâtre*, vol. 1, Paris: Gallimard, 1953.

becomes "Why did he put that there?" or "Why should (or does) that go there?" or "How does that fit in with this and this?"

But it is Heidegger who shows us most clearly the relation of purpose and pattern to meaning. For Heidegger man is essentially a being whose existence is to understand and interpret himself and his world. "*Dasein* is an entity which, in its very Being, comports itself understandingly toward that Being." [2] This basic feature of man Heidegger calls his Being-in-the-world. Man is the kind of thing which must live in a familiar, humanly interpreted world. Man is in the world not in the spatial sense in which a pea is in the pod, but in the sense in which one resides in familiar surroundings. Man is not plunked down in the midst of physical objects and primary substances, which he then goes on to try to make sense of. To speculate about physical objects or substance, to speculate at all, or even to *be* a human being, presupposes a recognizable world familiar to man answerable (even if negatively) to his needs and interests. Being-in-the-world, then, is composed of various human concerns. Our having a world, that is, one which we recognize and accept as our own, presupposes our being able to relate to objects in terms of our interests and needs, being able to see them as objects which can meet or thwart those needs. These concerns include "producing something, attending to something, looking after it, making use of something," [3] and even negatively, of neglecting or renouncing something.

This is the basis for our understanding of the world. More specialized and developed forms of knowledge arise out of and are articulations of this basic interpretative character of man, his being-in-the-world. Thus, the primary relation with a world is not, as traditional epistemology suggests, a bare perceptual grasp, a kind of intellectual staring, but a practical concern which "manipulates things and puts them to use" [4] in the implicit knowledge I have described as being-as. In our everyday attitude we see things as tools, instruments "for writing, sewing, working, transportation, measurement;" things are "essentially 'something in-order-to ...'." [5] Thus we project from our human standpoint a purposive relation on things, fixing them as means to some human end, an "*assignment* or *reference* of something

[2] Heidegger, Martin, *Being and Time* (John Macquarrie and Edward Robinson, trans.), London: S.C.M. Press, 1962, p. 78.

[3] *Ibid.*, p. 83.

[4] *Ibid.*, p. 95.

[5] *Ibid.*, p. 97.

to something." [6] We understand a pencil, for example, by relating it to the purpose or end of writing; this is how it can take a place in the phenomenal world of our concern. Normally, of course, this assignment of means to end is implicit, unnoticed; like being-as generally, it becomes apparent only by its loss. We become aware of the utility of the pencil, for example, just when we can't find it.

But any given purposeful relation is conceivable only as a part of a *system* of such relations. The pencil in order to write, writing in order to express ideas, convey a message, announce an intention, etc. This teleological chain can only be traced back so far; at some point one can only offer as the reason or end that this is "human nature" or our "form of life." And the whole complex of by-means-of, in-order-to relations forms the coherence structure, or meaning, of the world.

It is this projected, purposive understanding of his world which, on Heidegger's view, differentiates man from all other creatures. The difference between a man's "existence" and the "reality" of a stone is that the stone has no conception or concern with its being, with what it is and how it stands in relation to a world of other objects, which is the hall-mark of man's "existence." Because man's existence is "an issue" for him, "his existence has the basic character of *for the sake of*." [7] Man is a purposeful being, doing one thing for the sake of some desired end, and he is able to understand things and to have a "world" because he can project this purposive attitude on to the world. To exist, in this sense, is to be aware of (or capable of being aware of) possibilities, conceivable but unrealized alternative means to the same end, which the stone is not. I understand things by projecting on to them these unrealized possibilities; the pen, the paper, the typewriter, the books, all these are seen as fulfilling ends, realizing unsatisfied needs and desires and in this way are able to occupy a specific place in my world with a definite shape, character and value. In everyday existence the world is disclosed in terms of fixed, conventional possibilities which one tends to identify with the "real nature" of things, and so we become absorbed and lost in a world of naively objective "fact," thus forgetting the interpretative character of this human achievement. When this happens, the being-as character of the world fades from sight and comes to occupy that

[6] *Ibid.*

[7] King, Magda, *Heidegger's Philosophy*, New York: Dell Publishing (Delta Books), 1964, p. 43.

self-opaque level of thought we may characterize, following Wittgenstein, "continuous being-as," or more simply, "projection."[8]

Meaning for Heidegger (*Sinn*) is that which makes being-as possible, "that wherein the understandability of something maintains itself ..., (that) in terms of which something can be conceived ... as that which it is." [9] How are we able to see a chair *as* a chair, what makes this possible? This meaning background, which Heidegger calls "horizon," consists in man's ability to relate to and see things in terms of possibilities for purposeful activity—a knife for cutting, a tree to build a house or a fire, to provide shade or a home for a god, etc. In other words, what makes meaning possible is this capacity of man for purposeful, practical activity.

Thus, the '*horizon*' of meaning is human purpose, which is also an important *kind* of meaning. But the basic *character* of meaning would seem to be this ability to *project* purpose on to the world. Meaning is transcendentally traceable to purpose, and this brings out the intentional or 'subjective' side of meaning so lacking in Richards' account. But the important point about purpose is not the psychological fact that men can entertain thoughts about what they want, but that man can see the external world *in terms of* his purposes. Purpose is important, in other words, primarily as an explanation of *being-as*. Although the source and root of meaning is purpose, the key to understanding meaning is interpretation and projection. Meaning we want to think of primarily as an understanding or interpretation of reality, and this points to two basic aspects of meaning, the "subjective" side of understanding and the "objective" side of the reality to which this understanding is directed. Meaning is an understanding *of* reality (primarily in terms of purpose) which together we call interpretation or projection (being-as).

Because of their paramount importance for our analysis, let us look more closely at the relationship between meaning as purpose or intention and meaning as projection or being-as. Etymologically there appear to be two early sources for the modern sense of meaning: 1) to say or tell and, later, to think, and 2) to intend. The root, in other words, seems to be something like, "to have in mind" ("tell us what you have in mind," or "what do you have in mind?") which

---

[8] Wittgenstein, Ludwig, *Philosophical Investigations* (G. E. M. Anscombe, trans.), New York: The Macmillan Co., 1953, p. 194 ff.

[9] Heidegger, *op. cit.*, pp. 370-371.

yields meaning both in the sense of how we understand or interpret something and also what we intend to do or convey through speech, both of which are what we "say" or "tell" in speech. Obviously, intention and interpretation are very closely related.

What we intend to convey through speech is generally what we understand of a situation, and knowing *what* someone has done, that is, knowing how to interpret his action, usually involves some understanding of his intention. Meaning is something *we* understand *of* reality; hence, projection or interpretation. The most overt form of projection, and the most easily understood, is purposeful human action. My action indicates how I interpret the situation and is determined for me by that interpretation; it is also my attempt to impose my wish or thought upon the world, to find within the world the answer to my needs or desires. And of course what I project in action is what I have first projected in thought and interpretation. On the other hand, the typical *expression* of interpretation or intention is speech. Hence, the oldest root of "meaning" is "to say or tell." "What do you mean?", "Tell us what you have in mind," "Tell us how you see it"—these go together.

Speech is generally understood as intended to articulate some interpretation. Knowing what he meant is knowing how he sees things and how he intends us to see them, and this involves knowing how he approaches the world purposively from his particular point of view. We ask what his speech meant in order to understand what *he* meant in order to understand the interpretation of the world expressed by the speech. "What did he mean?"—i.e., "What was his interpretation, or understanding of the event?", "What interpretation was he trying to express?", "What interpretation are we to put on his speech vis-à-vis his intentions?"

Forms of speech may be regarded, then, as ways of seeing the world, expressing and fixing a disclosure or revelation of being-as. We are not normally aware of this unless the speech is original and fresh, as in poetry or some powerful theological or sociological concept, or perhaps a striking metaphor. Only then do we see speech *as* interpretative, as projecting an understanding of the world. Later, of course, this same line of poetry or brilliant metaphor will harden through repeated usage into a lifeless cliché. It is still disclosing reality, making it known to us, but we are no longer aware of the disclosure. The speech is still revealing being-as, but only "*continuous* being-as." And, of course, an important function of poetic and philosophic language is to jog us out of this disclosure-blind, lethargic acceptance of language and to present new aspects of the world from a fresh perspective, as Coleridge saw very clearly in relation to poetry,

awakening the mind's attention from the lethargy of custom, and directing it to the loveliness and the wonder of the world before us; an inexhaustible treasure, but for which, in consequence of the film of familiarity and selfish solicitude we have eyes, yet see not, ears that hear not, and hearts that neither feel nor understand.[10]

But whether "dawning" or "continous", whether conscious or blind, speech is a form of interpretation or projection.

This, then, is how we want to understand meaning, primarily as a form of understanding, interpretation or projection—as being-as and not, except derivatively, as the deciphered translation meaning of symbols. The main reason meaninglessness remains intellectually obscure is that it has traditionally been treated simply as a vacuously unfulfilled assignment of identity meaning to conventional, primarily linguistic symbols, rather than the loss of the familiar, interpreted world we recognize as our own—as though a meaningless life lacked meaning in the same empty way a nonsense word like "brillig" lacks meaning. The position I wish to develop on the other hand, is that we must look to projection and being-as to explain, beyond a superficial level, the meaningfulness and meaninglessness of language, as well as the modern psychological sense of meaninglessness described by the Existentialists. Existential meaninglessness consists in the realization that the meaning we find in the world is a human projection or accomplishment, and not something possessed by the world. In order to understand *this* sense of meaninglessness, we must first try to understand that sense of *meaning* the *lack* of which we experience as meaninglessness; viz., projection, or being-as.

In what sense, then, and to what extent *is* meaning a form of interpretation or projection? Projection is primarily a blind interpretation, an unselfconscious understanding of things, or as I said before, "continuous being-as." This definition turns on two basic elements: 1) the fact that it *is* an interpretation or way of seeing the world from a human point of view, and 2) the fact that we are *unaware* that this is an interpretation. Projection is not just seeing that some part of reality could be interestingly explored from a certain point

[10] Coleridge, S. T., *Biographia Literaria*, vol. 2 (J. Shawcross, ed.), London: Oxford University Press, 1962, p. 6.

of view; it is the *attachment* of this point of view to the *world* and a failure to see that it *is* a human point of view. The self-opaqueness of projection is brought out by the fact that it is generally a term used to describe *another's* view of the world and not one's *own*. I judge that *he* is reading into events his own biases, preferences, and interests; whereas I see myself as simply reading off objective characteristics of the situation as a druggist reads off the labels from his bottles of medicine and ointment. As we saw in Rickman and Rankin, projection is a term favored by psychologists and anthropologists for referring to other people's (generally false) conceptualizations and rationalizations of the world. Occasionally I do see myself as projecting, but then, for reasons we will discuss in the next and subsequent chapters, I see this as a mistake or error for which I am disappointed and sorry and which I try in future to avoid. Or, if I see myself as being under a constant illusion which I can neither correct nor abandon, then I become depressed and feel trapped in this illusion.

It is projection which enables us to get interested and finally absorbed in the world. We identify our meanings with the world and are thereby drawn into it, losing ourselves in it. In Wild's discussion projection is presented as the ordinary, naive unity of being and meaning, seeing meaning as a necessary and inseparable part of being, or rather, since it is never quite so explicit as this in everyday life, the failure to distinguish meaning from being. Thus projection must be naively blind; as soon as we see the meaning as ours, the meaning begins to separate itself off from being, and this divorce of being and meaning is what we call and experience as meaninglessness. The *awareness* of projection is the experience of meaninglessness. Hence, the central thesis of the book, the irony that if meaning is a form of projection, then meaninglessness is an awareness of the nature of meaning.

We have already noticed various applications of this idea of meaning as a human projection. In Camus absurdity is the experience of a world suddenly stripped of human meanings.

In a universe suddenly divested of illusion and lights, man feels alien, a stranger ... . At the heart of all beauty lies something inhuman, and these hills, the softness of the sky ... lose the illusory meaning with which we had clothed them.[11]

Compare this with Nietzsche.

[11] Camus, Albert, *The Myth of Sisyphus* (Justin O'Brien, trans.), New York: Vintage Books, 1960, pp. 5, 11.

All the beauty and sublimity with which we have invested real and imagined things I will show to be the property and product of man ... . O, the regal liberality with which he has lavished gifts upon things! Hitherto this has been his greatest disinterestedness, that he admired and worshipped and knew how to conceal from himself that he it was who had created what he admired.[12]

Ionesco also describes the meaningful world as a world of projected meanings, the loss of which is experienced either as the emptiness of things devoid of character or shape, or the leaden heaviness of mere "things" devoid of humanly understood meanings. And this, of course, is what Sartre describes as the feeling of nausea. In Genet we saw a vision of man trapped in the solitude of his own baseless projections, throwing up meanings against the walls of his own mind.

Now let us take a closer look at projection. To what extent is our own view of the world a projection and how do we become aware of it as projection? This presents an interesting methodological problem. It is part of the definition of projection that it be blind to itself; how then can and do we become aware of it? As in Heisenberg's "Principle of Indeterminacy," as soon as we become aware of it, it ceases to exist. Indeed, all our dealings with the world, which draw us into and tie us to a world, are engaged in a largely successful campaign *against* this awareness. The situation is not, however, quite so hopeless as it might seem. As I have suggested, projection is universal, but it is capable of degrees of transparency which represent the various stages of our awareness of it. As I said, we tend to see projection in others, and this is always understood against the background of nonprojected meaning. Thus, we see the more obvious forms of projection, say in the Olympian deities, or a childish explanation. But this becomes the thin edge of the wedge; from here we may go on to discover more and more examples of projection of a more and more fundamental kind, getting closer and closer to us, as it were, until we are led to the conclusion that *everything* we experience of the world is a humanly projection interpretation. And, in the absence of anything with which to contrast nonprojected meaning, the sense of projection is gradually shifted in the process until we come at last to the rather different sense of continuous being-as.

[12] Nietzsche, Friedrich, *The Will to Power* (A. M. Ludovici, trans.), in: *The Complete Works of Friedrich Nietzsche* (Oscar Levy, ed.), vol. 15, New York: Russell and Russell, 1964, p. 247.

From a few examples of subjective deviations from the norm, we are finally led to a new theory of meaning in general. Similarly in psychology, seeing-as was first introduced to account for certain deviant cases of seeing, and only later did it come to suggest a new theory of perception, the view that *all* seeing is seeing-as. At first we tend to assume that meaning is an inherent part of reality, and so we interpret all cases of seeing-as, or being-as as mistakes. Later as we begin to see that being-as infects practically all of our thinking about the world, we are led to the skeptical conclusion that we can't know anything. Finally, and this is what I am arguing for, we may come to understand seeing-as as a general account of how we do perceive things and being-as as a general theory of the way in which things do have meaning, and then the pessimistic and skeptical note largely vanishes. But this can happen only gradually and by degrees.

To a certain extent this gradual awareness has already taken place on a broad cultural plane. I assume, for example, that the world of the pre-Socratic Greek was a more meaningful (i.e., more coherent) world than the metaphysical world of Aristotle and St. Thomas which was itself a far more meaningful world than the scientific materialism of the 19th century. In other words, we can say that philosophers and scientists have been at work for centuries on this problem of projection—searching it out and eliminating it wherever they found it, progressively stripping the world of humanly projected meanings until they arrived at—what? Ideally, the hard core of reality, the thing itself; in actual fact, the modern experience of meaninglessness.

Accordingly, let us approach the question of projection by retracing our cultural steps, so to speak, starting from the historical "middle position" of the metaphysical world view of the Greek and Scholastic philosophers, which is both somewhat remote from us while still comprising a large part of our mental equipment. This, let us say, is about half way between the mythological or early theological construction of the world, which we all readily see as a human projection, and the modern positivist or scientific world view which, being both more "objective" and closer to us, may be more difficult to see as projection. This will give us some idea how a metaphysical or scientific view can, on the one hand, be an attempt to expose and transcend projection, and at the same time, in hindsight, be itself a form of projection. This will perhaps give us a better lever for dealing with views of the world closer in time to our own, seeing them, that is, in relation to their philosophical antecedents and placing them in a broad philosophical tradition of which we are the heirs. Gradually, the ubiquitous character of projection should become clear. This discussion should also make clear how every attempt to block the projection of humanly oriented concepts has simply channelled them into more remote but no less anthropomorphic forms. In Chapter 3 we will analyse this obsession, throughout Western philosophy, to strip off the layers of projected meaning to get down to the "thing itself" which in effect simply strips the world of meaning, leaving it meaningless.

The metaphysical world view of traditional philosophy is already a step toward the modern positivist and nihilistic loss of meaning. But looking at it in this way, say, by contrast with early Greek and Egyptian cosmologies, we may lose sight of how humanly oriented this metaphysical view was. Certainly, it is more abstract, more systematic, less dependent on theological suppositions, but it is nonetheless a human ordering of the world from a distinctly human point of view. In this sense it provides a glimpse of a relatively meaningful world, the loss of which from the 18th to the 20th century has been characterized by the modern experience of meaninglessness.

In what sense was the metaphysical world view more meaningful than the scientific? Or, since this comes to the same thing, in what sense was "the world of the pre-Socratic Greek a more meaningful world than the metaphysical world of Aristotle and St. Thomas?" Abraham, in *The Mind of Africa*, argues that "primitive" forms of thought (i.e., pre-metaphysical) are more, rather than less, rational than their metaphysical and post-metaphysical counterparts.[13] In what sense? In the sense that they include in a tightly knit system of thought a broader spectrum of human responses and relationships to the world—emotional, volitional and perceptual, as well as cognitive. As Frankfort, *et al.*, confirm in *Before Philosophy*, later metaphysical, "rationalistic," scientific views tended to be more and more abstract, and thus, cut off from the volitional, perceptual and emotional side of human nature, they became more irrelevant and coincidental and hence less rational.[14] In a mythological frame-

[13] Abraham, Willie, *The Mind of Africa*, Chicago: University of Chicago Press, 1962.

[14] Frankfort, H., Frankfort, H. A., Wilson, John A. and Jacobsen, Thorkild, *Before Philosophy*, Harmondsworth, England: Penguin Books, 1951.

work, for example, one is not satisfied with generalized explanations, for this leaves too much to chance. To say that a person died because of leukemia leaves out of account why this particular disease happened to attack this particular person at this particular time? If it is answered that he was more prone to the disease for various reasons, then the question remains why others similarly prone did *not* get it. If certain meterological conditions "cause" rain, why have these conditions come together at this particular time, say, of badly needed rains? If the man died from a stone falling on his head, why did that particular stone happen to fall just as the man was passing by? It is not enough to attribute this to chance or coincidence. Being more rational, mythological thought demands a sufficient and not just a necessary cause. As explanation becomes more general, it becomes more abstract and hence more circumstantial in relation to particular cases. The causes of the stone's falling and the causes of the man's walking along the path at that moment are unrelated and disconnected, and cannot be otherwise if the explanation is to be sufficiently general. What had been an ordered pattern of thought in the mythological context disintegrates into a collection of unrelated, compartmentalized systems. If someone asks today, "Why was my child born a mongol?" we are unable to provide an answer, even a bad one; we can only cop out by persuading the parent that the question is somehow out of place. But is it? It is in this sense that we may say, with Abraham and Frankfort, that the more scientific and intellectual the system, the less rational it is. And if mythology is in this sense more "rational" than metaphysics, then by the same token metaphysics is more "rational" than science. This is the sense in which Whitehead describes the greater rationality of medieval thought vis-à-vis that of the new science.

Galileo keeps harping on how things happen, whereas his adversaries had a complete theory as to why things happen ... . It is a great mistake to conceive this historical revolt as an appeal to reason. On the contrary, it was through and through an anti-intellectualist movement. It was the return to the contemplation of brute fact; and it was based on a recoil from the inflexible rationality of medieval thought.[15]

In so far as meaning is viewed as the systematic interrelatedness of parts within a whole, it follows that Galileo's world is less meaningful.

---

[15] Whitehead, Alfred N., *Science and the Modern World*, New York: Mentor Books, 1958, p. 9.

The consequent alienation of men from such a system of thought has been described from the time of the Romantic revolt in the 19th century to that of the Existentialists in the 20th. When the world is no longer accountable in emotional, perceptual, volitional terms, then it becomes strange to me and I find myself cut off from, no longer able to see anything in, nature that is mine.

Judged, then, from the mythological, pre-philosophical point of view, the traditional metaphysical world view is already a step toward the alienation and meaninglessness of the modern technological outlook. Overtly volitional, emotional, perceptual, anthropomorphic characteristics were systematically removed from the "objective" world and relegated to the "subjective" human sphere. But from the standpoint of modern science, this same metaphysical world comes across as a world rich in human meanings, a world we can understand and feel at home in. After all, it does adequately represent man's cognitive nature; it is accountable at least to man's intellect. Moreover, it still contains sublimated, rationalized references to volitional and emotional streams of meaning.

In this respect there is something to Comte's thesis, however facile in its extremity, that philosophy inevitably progresses through three distinct phases, the theological phase in which everything is viewed through decidedly human concepts of life and will, a metaphysical phase which substitutes abstractions for personal will but is still tied to quasi-volitional and religious absolutes, and the positivist phase which completes the process, setting aside the vain search for absolutes for a technologically more rewarding outlook.[16] What is harder to accept is Comte's conclusion that these three stages represent the progressive ascent to Truth, although even this, by its very exaggeration, lays bare the assumption that any projection is necessarily an anthropomorphic distortion which must be cast off to reveal the objectively real nature of things.

More specifically, how does traditional metaphysics project human values? First, in some rather obvious ways. Take, for example, the idea of a law of nature. It is fairly easy to see the idea of nature "obeying laws" as a projection of the human concern with social and political legislation. Roman philosophers held that things were governed by an inexorable law decreed by God, an idea transformed

---

[16] Comte, Auguste, *Cours, The Positive Philosophy of Auguste Comte* (Harriet Martineau, trans.), London, 1853.

in the Middle Ages into the quasi-political concept of a natural world governed by Divine commands. As Dewey put it,

We often hear about laws which 'govern' events, and it often seems to be thought that phenomena would be utterly disorderly were there not laws to keep them in order. This way of thinking is a survival of reading social relationships into nature ... the relation of ruler and ruled, sovereign and subject. Law is assimilated to a command or order. If the factor of personal will is eliminated (as it was in the best Greek thought) still the idea of law or universal is impregnated with the sense of a guiding and ruling influence exerted from above on what is naturally inferior to it.[17]

The abstraction of a law of nature from the phenomenon it governs is brought into sharp focus in Whitehead's famous analysis of Natural Law as imposed from the outside in a deliberative, "political" sense.

The explanation of the doctrine of Imposition both suggests a certain type of Deism, and conversely it is the outcome of such a Deistic belief ... . For example, we know from Newton's own statement that ... he definitely states that the correlated modes of behaviour of the bodies forming the solar system require God for the imposition of the principles on which all depended ... . He certainly thought that the conception of the solar system exhibited in his Principia was sufficiently ultimate to make obvious the necessity of a God imposing Law. Newton was certainly right to this extent, that the whole doctrine of Imposition is without interest apart from the correlative doctrine of a transcendent imposing Deity. This is also a Cartesian doctrine ... . It follows from ... Deism ... that the Laws of Nature will be exactly obeyed. Certainly, what God meant he did ... .[18]

Here, the idea of purpose and intention implied in issuing laws and commands comes out clearly. In order to control events and direct them to his own ends, God has chosen to enact certain laws which natural phenomena must obey. The idea of purpose projected into nature is still more prominent in the philosophic and scientific concern with final causes and teleological explanation. Human action is accounted for, in part at least, by intentional or deliberative reasons. "Why did you do that?" is usually a request for a purposeful *reason* rather than a physical or unconscious *cause*. And it seems clear to most of us today that explaining natural phenomena in this way, especially when theistic beliefs are put in the background, is a projection on reality of human ways of thinking and acting. As Whitehead rather picturesquely put it,

[17] Dewey, John, *Reconstruction in Philosophy*, New York: Mentor Books, 1950, p. 69.

[18] Whitehead, Alfred N., *Adventure of Ideas*, New York: Mentor Books, 1950, p. 115 ff.

The Greek view of nature ... was essentially dramatic ... . It thus conceived nature as articulated in the way of a work of dramatic art, for the exemplification of general ideas converging to an end. Nature was differentiated so as to provide its proper end for each thing ... . Nature was a drama in which each thing played its part.[19]

In Aristotle this idea was rationalized as the final cause, or entelechy of each thing according to its kind. Aristotle's basic distinction of form and matter is understood primarily in terms of the ends to be achieved by each member of the species. *What* a thing is, its being or essence (form), is determined by what that thing "strives" to achieve. Form is simply the completed stage of this entelechy. This comes out more clearly in the dynamic version of the distinction, that between potentiality (matter) and actuality (form). A thing exists potentially in the sense of what it *can* achieve and it exists actually in the sense of what it *has* achieved. But in either case it is understood in terms of an achievement which is itself explicable only in terms of intention and purpose. Not that Aristotle held an animistic belief in conscious wills inhabiting inanimate objects. But however rationalized or sublimated this idea of purpose may be, and however "subconscious" this purpose may have been conceived to be, it is only explicable, to use Kant's phrase, "purposively." Even if we deny to it conscious purpose, these are the terms in which we must understand it. Even the modern scientific concept of causality, like that of Natural Law, has its roots in the moral and legal justification of human action.

The priority of teleology as a supreme mode of explanation has always been recognized—no less, ironically, by Newton than by the Scholastics. On all sides it was agreed that if we are to explain things thoroughly, sufficiently, then we must employ final causes. The issue was whether one ought to give up final causality because of its incompatibility with the efficient causality of the new science. If Newton renounced teleological causes ("I propose no hypotheses"), it is only because he felt this would impede the progress of mechanical science;[20] and if Leibniz defended teleology, it is precisely on the grounds that

[19] Whitehead, *Science and the Modern World, op. cit.*, p. 8.
[20] Newton, Sir Isaac, *Scholium Generale* (A. Rupert Hall and Marie Boaz Hall, trans.), in: *Unpublished Scientific Papers of Isaac Newton* (Hall and Hall, ed.), Cambridge, England: Cambridge University Press, 1962, p. 360.

final causality does *not* impede, but completes, efficient causality.[21] Newton, of course, won the day, and teleology, and along with it sufficient reason, was the price paid for modern science.

For Plato the best form of explanation is in terms of the end or purpose for which each thing has been designed. In *Phaedo* and *Timaeus* two types of explanation are put forward: one in terms of mechanically necessary conditions and the other in terms of intelligent action for the sake of some good or desired end. In both these dialogues and elsewhere Plato argues that the former provides only a secondary or auxilliary cause, while the latter offers a *sufficient* explanation. To say that Socrates is sitting in prison because of the position of bones and leg muscles is not to answer the question *why* he is sitting there. Of course, he couldn't be sitting if his bones and muscles were not so arranged; that is, we have succeeded in specifying one necessary condition for Socrates' sitting in prison. But what has been left out of account is any explanation of *why* his bones and muscles are so arranged, and this can only be given in terms of Socrates' purpose in being there.[22] This is for Plato the model for all reasoning in the best sense. To explain the rising of the sun in terms of the earth's or the sun's orbit is not to explain why there is this orbit. Of course, mechanically necessary causes can be offered for the existence of the orbit, and other causes for this cause, and so on. But what kind of explanation, if any, *could* satisfy this chain of causes finally and completely, except to say at some point that this was done for the best, or that it fitted into some grand design? [23]

This is also the basis of Leibniz' attack on mechanical causality, that it is at best secondary and auxiliary, that it never provides a sufficient account of why things are as they are. Sooner or later the only way to end the chain of why's is to introduce some final cause. If we are to have sufficient reasons, then we must have teleology. Newton and the philosophers of the enlightenment accepted this reasoning, but denied the consequent arguing, *modus tolens*, that if

[21] Leibniz, Gottfried, *The Principles of Natural Grace*, in: *Philosophers Speak for Themselves: From Descartes to Locke* (T. V. Smith and Marjorie Grene, ed.), Chicago: University of Chicago Press, 1957, pp. 324-326.

[22] Plato, *Phaedo*, in: *The Works of Plato* (Irwin Edman, ed.), New York: The Modern Library, 1928, pp. 161-166.

[23] Plato, *Timaeus* (Jowett, trans.), New York: The Liberal Arts Press, 1949, p. 29.

we have to give up teleology, then we will have to sacrifice sufficient explanation.

Even an enlightenment philosopher like Kant recognized the necessity of explaining things in biology in teleological terms. Even if we deny that each organ of the human body has been deliberately fashioned to serve the ends of the others we inevitably tend to describe bodily functions in these terms.[24] Biologically, locomotion and distance perception seem to fit neatly together in a purposive relation, and we tend to explain each for the sake of, or as though for the sake of, the other.

These are examples of rather overt forms of projection, seeing the physical world as an analogue of the human world of commands and purposeful behavior. But projection also occurs in a more subtle and also more fundamental way in practically all the underlying conceptions of Western philosophy. As Burnet points out, the thrust of traditional metaphysics has always been to counteract a pessimistic attitude toward change, projecting an ideal solution to a basic anxiety over what is transient and impermanent. The basis of Western philosophy can thus be seen as the quest for the "ageless," "deathless" ground of permanence underlying change.[25] Dewey characterizes all traditional philosophies as various "recipes for denying to the universe the character of contingency." [26] Reality is constantly being identified with what is sure, regular and finished. Aristotle and Kant admit change only as a second order of reality. Even the philosophers of change, Heracleitus, Hegel and Bergson, glorify the eternality and absoluteness of change. According to Dewey, this metaphysical bias is based on a *moral* preference for order and stability. "Reality" is a projection of man's desire for a permanent buffer of stability against the hazardous, precarious nature of existence.[27] Hence, the concept of Being as fixed and stable which appears again and again in marked contrast with change and flux: in Plato (Forms and sensibles), Aristotle (form and matter), Kant (noumena and phenomena), and generally, in the reality/appearance distinction. We long for

[24] Kant, Immanuel, *Critique of Judgment* (J. H. Bernard, trans.), New York: Hafner Publishing Co., 1951, pp. 228-231.

[25] Burnet, John, *Early Greek Philosophy*, New York: Meridan Books, 1960, p. 9.

[26] Dewey, John, *Experience and Nature*, Chicago: Open Court Publishing Co., 1926, p. 46.

[27] *Ibid.*

perfect being, forgetting that it is this very human longing which gives meaning to the ideal. Always in the history of philosophy unity, permanence, eternality, completeness and rationality are grouped together and opposed to multiplicity, change, sensuous desire and the temporal, partial and defective.

But metaphysics project human thought on to reality in a still more fundamental way. Throughout Western philosophy the criterion of reality has always been what can be thought. We can see this most clearly in the rationalist equivalence (or near equivalence) of Being and rationality. *A priori*, the concept of Being is determined by the law of contradiction, i.e., a criterion of thought becomes a criterion of reality. In Parmenides "what is" is limited to what can be thought and what can be thought is determined and limited by the law of contradiction—which he further misunderstands as limiting true statements to identity statements. Confusing the "is" of predication and the "is" of identity, Parmenides argues that "A is B" implies that A is not A, which is self-contradictory. Thus the only admissible form of statement is the identity statement, "A is A." From this follow all the other characteristics of Being: that it is uncreated, indestructible, indivisible, homogeneous, continuous, immovable and unchanging.[28] This became the standard definition of Being for practically all subsequent philosophy. As Burnet points out, whether this definition finds its locus in materialism or idealism, the basic idea is the same.[29]

In Plato this criterion is applied to the Forms. Plato's admission of matter, or sensible phenomena is only a concession to the fact that thought is not entirely adequate to the world as we actually find it; it is a concession to the irrational factor of experience, not to the nature of reality. This forms the main basis for Plato's distinction between reality and appearance. Reality is limited to what can be thought according to this logical criterion; when we discover that certain things don't fit this criterion, we call this "appearance." That is, we acknowledge its presence, but recognize at the same time that it falls short of our rationalist definition of Being. Similarly in Bradley, there are two criteria of Being, the principle of noncontra-

---

[28] Parmenides, *The Way of Truth*, in: *The Presocratic Philosophers* (G. S. Kirk and J. E. Raven), Cambridge, England: Cambridge University Press, 1960, pp. 269-278.

[29] Burnet, *op. cit.*, p. 182.

diction and the ability to "save the appearances." And this harks
back to Hegel's doctrine that the real is whatever is rational.[30]

Secondly, Being has traditionally been conceived as Idea or Essence,
that is, it has always been thought of as strictly correlative with the
idea or concept which we have of a thing. This is quite independent of
"subjective idealism" which is not so much a kind, as a *recognition*
(and misunderstanding), of projection. What, for Plato, *meets* the
criterion of Being? Only the idea, which is not at all surprising
considering that the criterion of Being is primarily a rational criterion
of thought! An apple changes from green to red and thus, according
to Greek logic, contradicts itself and so cannot be real. But the idea
or concept, *greenness*, is always green and never anything else;
not being implicated in the contradictory nature of change it is
therefore real. Ironically, what satisfies the definition of Being is
thought. It is a necessity of thought, not of reality, a subjective rather
than objective necessity, that we think in terms of fixed, unchanging
concepts which we are more or less successful in reading back into
the world. Projection in Plato is mistaking this subjective necessity
for an objective reality. Plato acknowledges that the pattern of
Forms is only imperfectly mirrored in the world of flux, that to
attribute this pattern to the flux is an exaggeration and an imposition.
But this does not lead, as it might, to an awareness of projection and
being-as; instead Plato sees the Forms as enjoying a real existence
quite independent of human thought. The equivalence of concept
and Form is shown again by the one-to-one correspondence between
the two; for every general concept there is a Form. The Form is the
concept objectified, and it is called real because it is tailor-made to fit
the logical criterion of Being, noncontradiction.

All disclaimers to the contrary, Aristotle accepts Plato's Forms as
the ultimate reality but tries to locate them within the individual
primary substances. It is true, Aristotle defines substance, the unit
of reality, as both matter and form, but the reality of matter, whether
formed or Prime Matter, is always understood in terms of its actual
or potential *form*. Basically, for Aristotle, as for Plato, only form or
essence is real, with the rider that there are degrees of reality from
God right down to the first "mixing" of form with Prime Matter.
Metaphysics Z makes it quite clear that reality is to be understood

[30] Bradley, F. H., *Appearance and Reality*, London: George Allen and Unwin,
Ltd., 1920, p. 136.

primarily in terms of *what* a thing is, its essence or form. This essence is always what we can understand of a thing, and is hence always correlative with its definition. Aristotle's conception of essence contains important suggestions about the nature of projection and being-as, but on the whole this is played down in favor of the projection-blind Platonic idea of essence as an objective, real thing.

In the contemporary period, Santayana's concept of essence is also basically Platonic. So, too, are Whitehead's "eternal objects." Again the criterion is self-identity (Butler: "Everything is what it is and not another thing"); [31] whatever is logically possible is an essence. Although Santayana and Whitehead consider essence only one factor in reality among others, they nonetheless take the Platonic and Aristotelian line that reality cannot be thought or explained except in terms of abstract, real essences. And, again, the suggestion is that what is abiding and "really real" in the material world is what makes it intelligible and understandable, i.e., essence.

Finally, philosophical projection can be seen in the traditional essence/existence distinction. Essence is what we can understand of a thing, but since no list, however long, of essential properties can ever be identical with the thing itself or differentiate a real from an imaginary thing, a distinction is drawn between *what* a thing is (how we understand or conceive it) and the fact *that* it is (its bare existence). The interesting thing, however, is that it seems impossible to state or even grasp what this difference is because what we can state is always what we understand and conceive of a thing and this, by hypothesis, is essence. Various concepts, such as space, time, matter, and sensation have been used at various times to try to make out the distinction between a real object (which has essence and existence) and an imaginary object (which has essence but no existence). Thus a real object is said to exist in space or to be composed of matter. But all such attempts ultimately fail because these concepts are meaningless in a purely existential sense. Space, time or matter *in itself* is for us a myth, a merely hypothetical entity, while conceptual space and time can house all sorts of imaginary objects fleshed out with imaginary matter. And so we are thrown back on the idea that whatever we call reality is idea, form or essence. This, of course, should have led to the recognition of projection, that being is being-as.

[31] Butler, Joseph, *Five Sermons*, New York: The Library of Liberal Arts, 1950, p. 15.

But instead it led either to Platonic realism, the doctrine that Ideas have a real existence independent of human thought, or to Berkelian idealism, that the world is in some sense an idea in my mind.

A partial exception is Bergson who realized the projective nature of *analytic* thought but held out for a direct realist theory of *intuitive* knowledge. All conceptual, analytic thinking, he maintains, is an imposition of human concerns on reality, simplifying, rearranging, and necessarily, distorting. Analytic, intellectual thought "depends on the point of view at which we are placed and on the symbols by which we express ourselves." [32] In this sense, he argues, analytic thinking simply "moves around" the object, focusing on certain aspects which this object shares with others, but leaving us always "outside" the object. "Symbols and points of view ... place me outside (it); they give me only what (it) has in common with others, and not what belongs to (it) and to (it) alone." But this is at best "a translation, a development into symbols, a representation." [33]

This does not mean that projection is an entirely worthless pursuit, however. In a practical sense it is not only useful but absolutely necessary for classifying objects into general, abstract kinds, without which we could neither think nor speak. The mistake lies in identifying the concept with the thing, the translation with what is being translated, or as the Zen Buddhists say, mistaking the pointing finger for the moon.

Concepts ...—especially if they are simple—have the disadvantage of being in reality symbols substituted for the object they symbolize ... . Examined closely, each of them ... retains only that part of the object which is common to it and to others, and expresses ... a *comparison* between the object and others which resemble it. But as the comparison has made manifest a resemblance, as the resemblance is a property of the object, and as a property has every appearance of being a *part* of the object which possesses it, we easily persuade ourselves that by setting concept beside concept we are reconstructing the whole of the object with its parts, thus obtaining, so to speak, its intellectual equivalent ... . There precisely is the illusion.[34]

The translation falls short in two respects; it is partial and it is abstract and general. The latter is expressed very nicely in Whitehead's *Fallacy of Misplaced Concreteness*, the "error of mistaking the abstract for the concrete." Mechanism, for example,

[32] Bergson, Henri, *An Introduction to Metaphysics* (T. E. Hulme, trans.), New York: The Liberal Arts Press, 1949, p. 21.

[33] *Ibid.*, pp. 22-24.

[34] *Ibid.*, p. 28.

is quite unbelievable. This conception of the universe is surely framed in terms of high abstractions, and the paradox [how the world appears so different] only arises because we have mistaken our abstractions for concrete realities.[35]

To take a very simple example, to say of a golf ball that it is round, white and hard is to describe it truthfully, but it is also to describe only a few of the many possible aspects under which it could be viewed and which could be truly applied to it (that it is dimpled, expensive, etc.), and it is also to break it up (i.e., "analyse" it) into a series of generalized features which it shares with many other things (white fences, round melons, and hard biscuits). We can never offer more than such a list of partial, abstract features and yet no finite list of such features can ever exhaust the thing, or can be identical with it. In this sense the golf ball never just *is* a round, white, hard ball, despite the fact that this is a perfectly accurate and true description. As we saw in our discussion of the essence/existence distinction, a list, however long, of abstract, general qualities never seems to fix the simple unique object. It is a mistaken view of language and the nature of human thought to suppose that it *should* fix the object in this way.

It is the very utility of conceptualization which, on Bergson's view, renders it inherently incomplete and inaccurate. The whole point of conceptualization is to fasten on to relatively stable aspects of things which we can represent to ourselves and in terms of which we can classify and relate other objects in various ways. But by this very token we are constantly falsifying the continuous, fluctuating, transient character of things.

Our mind, which seeks for solid points of support, has for its main function in the ordinary course of life that of representing *states* and *things*. It takes, at long intervals, almost instantaneous views of the undivided mobility of the real. It thus obtains *sensations* and *ideas*. In this way it substitutes for the continuous the discontinous, for motion stability, for tendency in the process of change, fixed points marking a direction of change and tendency. This substitution is necessary ... to positive science.[36]

Bergson takes us to the brink of realizing that all thought is projection, all being being-as, but he never quite steps over that brink. Throughout, Bergson characterizes projection as a distortion or

---

[35] Whitehead, *Science and the Modern World, op. cit.*, p. 56.
[36] Bergson, *op. cit.*, p. 50.

falsification, and this implies some *nonprojective* understanding which does *not* falsify or place us outside the object, but which penetrates to its very nature. For Bergson, of course, this is intuition, a nonconceptual, direct grasp of reality. As we will see later, even in Nietzsche's pessimistic rejection of *all* forms of thought as projection, there is still the implied contrast with a nonprojected source of understanding which directly grasps the thing itself.

But isn't this idea of a nonprojective understanding itself a form of projection? What would a nonprojective form of understanding be like? It would have to be a comprehension or understanding which was also somehow identical (at least in essence) with the thing itself. And this presupposes the concept of the essential nature of the thing itself. But do objects possess essential attributes in and of themselves, independently of all human thought, or is this not itself a form of projection, indeed the ultimate form of projection?

Like most philosophers, Bergson has followed the argument part of the way, but not all the way. The argument begins naively with the assumption that meaning is identical with reality, that projection is error. Bergson presses on beyond this naive beginning, coming to the realization that projection is necessary to our knowledge of reality. But this leads him to the conclusion that we don't really know anything (at least conceptually where he sees projection to be operative), a conclusion which presupposes the old identities of meaning and reality, projection and error. For Bergson's argument, if it makes any sense at all, runs something like this. If knowledge is defined as the identity of thought with its object, then we are incapable of knowledge just to the extent that thought must impose (project) an interpretation on the object. And here Bergson, like most philosophers, stops. But the *argument* doesn't end here at all. If projection is a necessary part of meaning and knowledge, then the initial premise in the above argument is false (i.e., knowledge is *not* the identity of thought with its object), and the conclusion, which Bergson is unable to draw, ought to be that projection is the *nature* of meaning and knowledge, that there is as much meaning to the world as there is projection, that the world is meaningful just in so far as it is interpreted.

When we look at the kinds of projected meaning we have been examining, we see that they fall broadly into two main groups—the idea of essence and the idea of thinghood; either the distinct, permanent, self-identical thing itself, independent of thought, underlying

properties and change, or the essential nature of a thing identical
with and inseparable from that thing itself. The experience of meaninglessness, and also the awareness of projection, has been defined
precisely as the separation of these two, the alienation of any comprehensible essence from the thing itself. What I want to stress now is
that both of these notions are projections, and moreover, that they
are the bases of most of the other philosophical projections and the
ones most difficult to grasp.

Reality has always been conceived in terms of thinghood. What is
real is the thing as it is in itself, that is, independent of any projected
interpretation, or thought. Interestingly, both Ryle and Heidegger
complain that the concept of real Being has been given over entirely
to the object. Traditionally, if X is not an object or an inseparable
part of an object, then it is not real. And if it *is* real, then it is a thing,
an object. Hence, either the alleged unreality of secondary qualities
and mental states, or else the attempt, for example in Descartes,
to think of mind as a non-physical *object*. With the pre-Socratics and
even with Plato and Aristotle, anything real, even a principle such
as Love or Strife, or a universal or essence, was thought to be some
kind of entity or object. This, of course, arises out of the common
sense view of the world as composed of solid, three-dimensional,
semi-permanent things which *are* just as they *appear*. But it is nonetheless a projection. The idea of a permanent, unchanging substance,
whether in philosophy or common sense, is at best a simplification,
abstraction, extrapolation or rounding off, primarily for convenience
in naming, classifying, and conceptualizing. As Strawson points out
in *Individuals*, it is a *conceptual and linguistic* necessity that we think
of the world as composed of discrete, semi-permanent objects inhabiting a fixed spatio-temporal environment.

But we also think of reality as having some comprehensible *nature*
which we don't read into it. This is identified in an unclarified way
with the thing itself; it is what the thing *is* in itself. But being comprehensible, it is also correlative with our ideas or thoughts. Hence,
it is a definable essence or meaning.

Traditional metaphysics has always vacillated between these two
conceptions of reality. On the one hand, reality is the thing itself
—stripped of all essence, meaning, interpretation, quality, etc.
(Locke's substratum or Aristotle's "Prime Matter"); but reality is
also *what* a thing is, its classifiable, intelligible nature which it shares
in common with other things (Aristotle's secondary substance or

essence or Descartes' attributes). Reality is the thing itself, but it is also *what* that thing *is*.

Thus, the kind of meaning we project on the world which ultimately opposes being-as is the notion of thinghood and idea, and the curious dialectical relationship between them. Like two sides of a coin, each presupposes the other. When we think of reality we think of a thing or things. But what exactly do we mean by this? We mean something substantial, that is, unchanging, self-identical, self-subsistent. But what will answer to such an extreme notion? Ironically, only an idea, or concept. On the other hand, when we think of reality we think of *what* the thing is, its essence. But when we try to define the nature of this essence we tend to conceive it as an entity, or thing, like Plato's "Universals," Santayana's essences or Whitehead's eternal objects. In practice our ideas may not be adequate to things, but our *concept* of idea is tailor-made to fit our *concept* of thing.

Historically, these two opposed concepts of reality have become completely entwined in one another in a hopeless tangle. When we think of the thing-in-itself, we tend to think of a thing whose essence is identical with itself (Aristotle's primary substance or Descartes' corporeal substance with the attribute extension). What the concept thus demands is a nature which we can comprehend but which is not in any way subjective or interpretive, in other words, an interpretation which is not interpretative. How is such a thing possible? Ultimately confused and irrational, it nonetheless lies at the heart of all our attempts to discover the real, objective nature of things, casting off all projection and "subjective" interpretations. The root of the idea is the commonsense assumption (or attitude) that that thing over there just *is* a tree, that what we comprehend and grasp as a tree just is (is identical with) that thing. It is the tacit denial that treeness is a concept, that its being a *tree*, rather than a piece of wood, a canopy of shade, or a kingdom of elves, is a projection; a denial, in short, of interpretation and being-as.

Thus the final awareness of projection is the recognition that the real nature of the thing itself is a convenient myth, an operational or regulative concept, but not a possible item of experience or contemplation; in short, the ultimate projection. The recognition of this point has been forced upon recent philosophy in two quite distinct forms. The first is the discovery of the English-speaking Language Analysts that there cannot literally be any sense-data or atomic facts as these had been defined and conceived; that is, nothing expressible or comprehensible which is not also an interpretation from a limited human point of view. The second is the Phenomenologist's concern with man's absorption in a world of human projects and concerns, in which to have "a world" at all is to project meaning. We will want to look briefly at each of these in turn.

Traditional philosophy assumed, and this assumption is equally a part of common sense, that there must be one interpretation or meaning (the "essence") which is identical with and a part of (the "real nature" of) the thing itself. It was not that projected meaning was always *false*, but just that it *was* an interpretation and not the real nature of the thing. The mark of projection in relatively obvious cases is the falsity of the projection. Zeus does *not* hurl thunderbolts; therefore, it is projection to say that this is the cause of rain. But in those less obvious cases of concern to philosophers, the awareness of which leads to the charge that all thought is projection, the criterion becomes the subjective relativity of projected meanings. There are many different human points of view and sets of assumptions, all yielding more or less accurate information relative to that point of view and those assumptions.

This would have led to the conclusion that all thought is necessarily projective, were it not for the persistent idea that all of these more or less accurate, relatively truthful projections stand in opposition to the real nature of X which is *not* an aspect or interpretation and against which all the others are judged inferior. All projections are more less accurate and true, but they are also more or less inaccurate and false; and the idea persists that one should not settle for less than the absolute truth, i.e., a direct intellectual grasp of the real nature of the thing itself. The search for truth has therefore been conceived as the search for this real essence. Methodologically, this meant eliminating projected meanings until one reached the real nature of the thing itself. It was like peeling off the layers of an onion to get down to—what?

Empiricists employed this methodology in order to discover what we really *perceive*, the real percept stripped of all human interpretations, the bare empirical fact revealed directly and automatically through sensation. The method was to limit and by degrees to eventually eliminate the interpretative content of perception. If one claimed to hear a coach outside it was pointed out that this was an interpretation, that in greater accurancy the claim ought to be narrowed to hearing a coach-like sound and that even this must be further confined to the bare claim that one had the experience of what seemed an external sound of a coach-like nature. This procedure was directly correlative with the attempt to eliminate error, i.e., with the search for certainty. It was correctly seen that a necessary condition of error was interpretation. (What was not so readily seen was that this was also a necessary condition for truth.) Interpretation presumed to go beyond the data, predicting or anticipating what could not actually be seen at that moment. And this was the crack through which error could enter our perceptions. If I say, "I see a tomato," to take the philosopher's favorite example, I am "predicting" that if I were to bite into it, it would taste sweet and tart, have seeds, etc., or at least negatively that I would be surprised if this turned out *not* to be the case. But to do this is to stick one's neck out, to make oneself liable to be proved wrong by subsequent experience, for it might turn out to be a wax tomato or a vegetable of a different kind. So, the assumption was that to eliminate error and the possibility of error one must eliminate interpretation.

Similarly in Descartes' hats and coats example, we are inclined to say we seen men walking in the street below, but we can't actually see the men, covered as they are in hats and coats, and the consequent possibility of error, however small, points to the interpretative, hypothetical nature of such a judgment and forces a reduction to the claim that we at least see hats and coats moving about below.[37] But even this presumes too much. Perhaps, it's all a dream or an hallucination. Certainly (and this is the point of the dream hypothesis) it is a (possibly false) interpretation which goes beyond the bare data. But however difficult it was to specify what this bare datum was, it was nonetheless assumed that as we narrowed the claim from men-in-hats-and-coats, to hats-and-coats, to what-appeared-to-be-hats-and-coats, we were moving toward (getting down to) the bare perceptual facts where truth and certainty were assured.

Modern phenomenalists have translated this search for the basic real percept into a search for the ultimately uninterpreted, merely factual *description* of sensedata, a linguistic description, in other words, which asserted no more than, nor presumed to go one jot beyond, what was simply given in sensation. Rather than reducing ordinary perceptions to sense data, they were thus concerned to

[37] Descartes, Rene, *Meditations*, in: *Descartes Selections* (Ralph Eaton, ed.), New York: Charles Scribner's Sons, 1955, p. 104.

reduce *statements about* ordinary perceptions to *statements about* sense data. The latter were called "protocol" or "atomic" propositions, and our story concerns the trials and tribulations of those philosophers, the Logical Atomists or Positivists, who labored in vain for years, trying to find the magic formula which would express the empirical content of bare sense data without simultaneously introducing interpretive content. Eventually it was seen that the terms in which the problem was stated were self-contradictory, that in so far as empirical content was expressible at all, it was to that extent an interpretation, that the more one reduced interpretation, the more one reduced the meaning of empirical statements so that the hypothetical lower limit of no interpretation would be a statement with no meaning. In short, it was seen that you couldn't have meaning without interpretation, and therefore you couldn't have any protocol or atomic propositions. The limits of interpretation turned out to be the limits of meaning and this led to the brink of the realization that meaning and thought are essentially interpretation and projection.

The first major assumption of the early logical analysts was that linguistic meaning is based on the structural similarity between sentence and fact.[38] In Logical Atomism, and later in Logical Positivism, a proposition was true if and only if it corresponded with an atomic fact of the world. In the *Tractatus* Wittgenstein had already recognized that the atomic elements corresponding to statements must be construed as facts rather than objects. This perception was really the beginning of the end for Logical Atomism, for a fact is already an intelligible, descriptive aspect of the world, a unit of meaning, however basic. Russell had tried to treat the proposition and the fact as molecular, that is, as a list of names denoting objects, properties and relations. But Wittgenstein saw that this was insufficient; he recognized that a proposition was a conventional, human way of *taking* and relating these things, and that these entities could not be meaningfully referred to by anything less than a descriptive, factual assertion. Thus, so far as language was concerned, they did not exist on their own but only as part of the fact *that* such and such is the case. "The white cat" is not just the name of a thing and a property;

---

[38] Urmson, J. O., *Philosophical Analysis*, Oxford: Clarendon Press, 1956, pp. 18-21.

it is an assertion of the fact that the cat is white and thus an interpretation or way of seeing the world.[39]

At first the Atomists tried to construe the relation of proposition to
fact as the presumably simple and mechanical (i.e., nonintentional)
relation of naming or denoting. The motive behind this move was to
get as far as possible from the subjective element of interpretation.
A proposition did nothing to the fact; it simply named it or called
attention to it, leaving it otherwise alone. But Wittgenstein saw that
this would not do, for more than one proposition can refer to the
same fact; if the reference to facts is simply one of naming, then each
fact has several names, which is absurd. The *Tractatus* is an attempt
to find a compromise relation which would skirt the extremes between
mechanical denoting and the conventional, interpretive character
of meaning. His solution was that propositions "pictured" facts.
A proposition depicted the relation between perceptual elements by
an *analogous* relation between linguistic elements, in the way the
spatial relation of lines and colors on a map, for example, reflects
the spatial relation of roads, rivers and mountains.[40] The point was
to avoid any reference to the conventional, interpretive nature of
language, to the fact that we use words intentionally for certain
purposes, as Wittgenstein later saw. Like Morris' notion of an "iconic
sign," [41] this idea of a "picture" was thought to do the trick. But,
of course, it does not. A map or representational picture is just as
conventional as a literary description of a town or landscape. It's
true that once you have got the convention, you know how to go
on interpreting new maps and pictures without learning new rules
and conventions. But it is nonetheless a convention. Wittgenstein
admits there is a rule for reconstructing the fact from the sentence-
picture, and this suggests convention, but the appeal of the picture
was nonetheless to minimize this conventionality.

The distinction Wittgenstein drew in the *Tractatus* between what
can be *said* and what can only be *shown* linguistically indicates the
chief weakness of the early Atomist theory of language. If the meaning
of language is a nonconventional picturing of the facts, then most
of what we say in nonsense, including any philosophic discussion,

---

[39] Wittgenstein, Ludwig, *Tractatus Logico-philosophicus* (D. F. Pears and
B. F. McGuinness, trans.), London: Routledge and Kegan Paul, 1963, pp. 21-23.
[40] *Ibid.*
[41] Morris, Charles, "Science, Art and Technology," in: *A Modern Book of
Esthetics* (Melvin Rader, ed.), Holt, Rinehart, and Winston, 1960, p. 245.

such as the *Tractatus*, of the relation of language to the world. To avoid castigating most of our language as nonsense, Wittgenstein proposed that language can also *show* us even what it cannot literally *state*.[42] The most likely candidate for the picturing, stating view of language is something like "The cat is on the mat." "Cat" names or refers to the cat, "mat" denotes the mat, and "is on" names the relation obtaining between the two. The proposition simply states this, "telling it like it is." But even granting this as an adequate account of "the cat is on the mat," it is hopeless to try to apply this analysis to statements like "art is expression," "money is the root of all evil," "only empirically verifiable statements are synthetically meaningful." These propositions don't pick out experienceable elements in the world and state how they are related. They attempt to show, or suggest a way of looking at things, a way of construing, judging, or handling things. They have *some* relation to the world of facts, but not the presumably direct one of naming things and their properties and the relations which obtain between them.

But this distinction simply provided the thin edge of the wedge, spelling the eventual downfall of the theory. As Wisdom saw, very few, if any, sentences state facts; most sentences sketch rather than picture facts, and "sketching" is really a kind of showing.[43] Once the distinction was granted, it gradually became clear how much of our language showed rather than stated, and more and more that had previously been understood as stating came to be seen as showing. Eventually, there was nothing left on the stating side of the distinction, which wrecked the distinction and the theory of language on which it rested. Applying the distinction became its most devastating critique.

We should be able to discover the same dialectical process taking shape as we press our analysis of projection, seeing it first as contrasting unfavorably with nonprojective forms of understanding, then recognizing more and more "nonprojective" forms of understanding as projection, resulting finally in a new appreciation and evaluation of the nature of projection. What I hope to do eventually is show that no proposition states or could state in the sense Wittgenstein suggests in the *Tractatus*, that all any proposition can do is to show, i.e., to indicate, point, or suggest.

[42] Wittgenstein, *op. cit.*, p. 51.

[43] Wisdom, John, "Logical Constructions (I)," *Mind*, vol. 40, no. 158, 1931, p. 202.

The second main assumption of the early analysts was the simple, unconventional, one-to-one relation between words and objects, *unum nomen, unum nominatum.* The meaning of a word was simply the thing it named or referred to. But what this referring consisted in was left unexplained; it was supposed to be an automatic, natural (i.e., unconventional), brute relation which required no explanation. The point of a logically proper name was that it didn't describe, or interpret the object at all; it simply named it. But as Ayer pointed out, "the fact is that one cannot in language point to an object without describing it." [44] This went to the core of the problem. To state a proposition, however elemental, is necessarily to say something *about* the object, to classify or describe it, and this is necessarily to go beyond the given.

It was for reasons of this sort that Wisdom doubted whether one could find an example of an atomic proposition. "This is red" does not just, or simply, (i.e., unconventionally, unintentionally) name or picture a fact. "This" means "the thing I am pointing to" and involves conventions as to the use of pointing in a linguistic context, while "red" refers to a conventional and rather arbitrary range of hues of varying densities and brightness, all of which goes well beyond the hypothetical given.[45] As Ayer put it, it is "not merely that no ostensive propositions are expressed, but that it is inconceivable that any ostensive propositions ever should be expressed." [46]

What Wittgenstein has done in *Philosophical Investigations* is to demonstrate in more detail and more persuasively the complete unworkability of the naming-meaning model. Even in a simple language in which words *do* refer to objects in a one-to-one relation, the referring is an institutionalized language game played according to conventional rules. Even naming (think of christening) is a conventional institution with prescribed rules (we name people but not chairs, we don't normally alter a person's name again and again). Thus, the emphasis in Wittgenstein's later philosophy on meaning as use, meaning, that is, in relation to social conventions, institutions and ways of life dictated by human needs and purposes.[47] Thus, analytic philosophers were led, however unwilling, to the conclusion,

[44] Ayer, A. J., *Language, Truth and Logic*, London: Golanz, 1936, p. 91.
[45] Wisdom, *op. cit.*, p. 203.
[46] Ayer, *op. cit.*
[47] Wittgenstein, *Philosophical Investigations, op. cit.*

or at least to the brink of the conclusion (since they never quite saw the entire point of their own discoveries) that all thought and meaning is projection.

It was left to the Phenomenologists, especially Husserl and Heidegger, to expose in greater scope and subtlety the full significance of projection as a universal phenomenon. In his discussion of the "natural attitude" Husserl was concerned to analyse the possibility of man's having a world as disclosed in the light of everyday, non-reflective experience, that is, the "world from the natural standpoint." The question is not whether and how there is a world, in the sense in which this would interest the physicist, but how it is possible for man to live and move about understandingly in a world which he comprehends, and how it is possible for the world to be experienced and understood in this way. Husserl's answer is the intentional nature of human thought, the fact that thought is always about, or always directed toward an object, i.e., some meaningful content standing over against the thinking subject.[48] To think, in other words, presupposes a world; "I think, therefore I have world." In Husserl's view, we have a world because we project meaning. But it is Heidegger's exhaustive application of this idea which is most relevant to our analysis of projection.

Unlike most metaphysical accounts, Heidegger's theory of Being is not built round the contrast between real and ideal or between reality and appearance. Heidegger contrasts both real *and* ideal, reality *and* appearance with nothingness. Being is therefore whatever can be comprended *as something* rather than substantial reality or thinghood which he regards as only one kind of Being, and a derivative kind, at that. Even fictional entities, dreams, and mirages I understand *as* something; I apprehend them as meaningful items in the world of my experience. Hence they *are* something; they have Being if not reality. Being for Heidegger, in other words, is being-as. As we saw earlier, nothingness is not the nonexistence of things (the absence of substantial thinghood), but the *meaninglessness of things*. A thing is real if it exists independently of my awareness of it, and a consideration of reality is important both to scientists and to traditional metaphysicians, but whether real or ideal it must first *be* something. Before the question of reality or appearance can arise

[48] Husserl, Edmund, *The Idea of Phenomenology* (William Alston and George Nakhnikian, trans.), The Hague: Martinus Nijhoff, 1964, p. 13.

the item in question must form part of a humanly meaningful world. As Husserl put it, all investigations, whether epistemological, metaphysical or scientific are directed at items of the world from the natural standpcint. Before there is anything to discuss philosophically or scientifically, there must first be a projected world of being-as. To investigate the reality or ideality of secondary qualities, such as color, for example, presupposes that there *is* something in our world experienced as color. If color did not belong to the everyday, pre-philosophical world, it could never get discussed by psychologists, physicists and physiologists. Thus, far from denying the being of colors, these scientific investigations confirm their existence in the world of everyday experience.

Much of Husserl's and Heidegger's thought is directed at establishing the right priorities between items as experienced in the world of everyday experience and as described by philosophers and scientists. They are opposed to the traditional view which first postulates the priority of substantial Being, whether matter or primary substance or scientific atomic substance, and then tries to reconstruct as much of the everyday world as possible from this. The history of modern philosophy can be seen as the gradual discovery that this was an impossible task. The point Husserl and Heidegger make is that the difficulty lies in the original supposition that substantial Being is primary, putting the cart before the horse. Substantial reality (the thing itself) is a philosophical refinement of everyday reality, proceeding from a particular human point of view which involves the metaphysical biases we saw earlier. Traditional metaphysics is based on the assumption that reality is synonymous with Being, the identification of meaning with reality which denies or obscures being-as. Thus, Heidegger has struck at the very foundations of this tradition by asserting that reality is only one kind, and not the only, or only genuine, kind of Being.

What the traditional priority of substantial reality and its identification with Being has done is to obscure the question of Being, the question, that is, why we have a comprehensible world at all, why there is something (in the sense of being-as) rather than nothing, and how it is possible that man can respond understandingly to a world and the world present itself to man as a meaningful item to be explored and investigated. Since substantial real Being is only one kind of Being, a satisfactory answer to the question of reality pre-supposes a satisfactory answer to the prior question of Being. But by identifying reality with Being and putting reality first, the question of Being (being-as) never gets raised; it is merely assumed or taken for granted and hence ignored. What traditional metaphysics obscured, ironically, is the Being of the world—and this means, in terms of our analysis, an understanding of the world as the projection of being-as.

Parallel with the mistaken priorities accorded Being and reality is the correlative ranking of philosophical, scientific or intellectual apprehension as prior to the everyday understanding of things. Substantial being is the product of a kind of intellectual staring, a way of knowing removed entirely from practical, emotional significance, a knowing for the sake of knowing, which reveals the traditional objects of metaphysical inquiry—ideas, essence, matter, substance, etc. Husserl's and Heidegger's point, and this has also been stressed by Dewey and Ryle, is that this intellectual staring arises out of, and would be impossible without, the absorbed, interested non-thematic everyday understanding. As mentioned earlier, everyday understanding is not always or usually a conscious or explicit analysis, but a continuous seeing-as, a sense of familiarity which is best described negatively. I walk into my office and perceive and behave understandingly toward the room and its contents. I hang up my coat, open the window, look at my mail, etc. But I do not think or say to myself, "This is a window; a window should be opened to let in air, etc."

For Heidegger, as we saw before, this tacit understanding is practical and purposeful. Things reveal themselves as meaningful items and we are thereby able to have a world because we can see them as projects for our own ends and designs; they are part of a world and make that world possible because they can become objects of our concern. This circumspective, practical understanding Heidegger describes as a kind of seeing-as.

We 'see' it *as* a table, a door, a carriage, or a bridge ... . Whenever we see with this kind of sight, we already do so understandingly and interpretatively. In the mere encountering of something, it is understood in terms of a totality of involvements and such seeing hides in itself the explicitness of the assignment-relations which belong to that totality.[49]

And it is from this that more explicit forms of understanding can arise. As understanding, *Dasein* projects its Being upon possibilities ... the

[49] Heidegger, *op. cit.*, p. 189.

projecting of the understanding has its own possibility—that of developing itself (which) we call 'interpretation,' ... the working out of possibilities projected in understanding.[50]

But what we explicitly interpret has already been implicitly understood. This is why we aren't normally aware of projection; it is too intimately involved in the very having of a world. The world arises with projection, and projection arises with human understanding. Like a man with very poor eye-sight, he is only aware of his glasses when he takes them off.

Thus it is man and his concerns which make Being (being-as) possible. Not that we create or invent the world, or that the world exists somehow in my head, but that the meaningful character without which there can be no comprehensible world only occurs in man's understanding relation to things. As Magda King puts it,

No animal, not even the highest, can treat a thing as the kind of thing it is ... . The world is not a thing, but man himself is worldish; he is ... world disclosing, world forming ... . Significance, i.e., the world, only 'is' in the understanding of man.[51]

Man is essentially world and meaning disclosing. To be a man is to live in a meaningful and partially understood world. Thus, meaning, truth, Being arise with the having of a world which is itself the product of man's projecting, absorbing understanding. Meaning is thus the human ground of the possibility of an intelligible world of being-as, and in this sense all meaning, for Heidegger, is projection.

In the projecting of the understanding, entities are disclosed in their possibility ... . Entities within-the-world generally are projected upon the world —that is, upon a whole of significance to whose reference-relations concern, as Being-in-the-world, has been tried in advance. When entities within-the-world ... have come to be understood, we say that they have *meaning* (*Sinn.*) But that which is understood, taken strictly is not the meaning, but the entity ... . Meaning is that wherein the intelligibility of something maintains itself ... . Meaning is the 'upon which' of a projection in terms of which something becomes intelligible as *something* ... . Meaning is an *existentiale* of *Dasein*, not a property attaching to entities ... . *Dasein* only 'has' meaning, so far as the disclosedness of Being-in-the-world can be 'filled in' by the entities discoverable in that disclosedness. *Hence, only Dasein can be meaningful or meaningless.* That is to say, its own Being and the entities disclosed with its Being can be appropriated in understanding, or can remain relegated to non-understanding.[52]

[50] *Ibid.*, p. 188.
[51] King, *op. cit.*, pp. 28, 73, 85.
[52] Heidegger, *op. cit.*, pp. 192-193.

This means that apart from human projection, things "must be conceived as *unmeaning*, essentially devoid of any meaning at all ... *and only that which is unmeaning can be absurd*." [53]

But the force of Heidegger's thought is not to *deny* that things are meaningful but only to discover what *makes* them thus. Heidegger would complete Bergson's argument. The world is meaningful *because* we project meaning. To argue from this that the world itself is meaningless is both to affirm *and* to deny that meaning is projection. The necessary condition for meaning is man's intentional, projecting understanding. To argue that the world is therefore really, in-itself meaningless is to reintroduce the priority of substantial Being, assuming, in other words, that the world can be meaningful only if meaning is an essential property of the substantial thing-in-itself. But substantial Being only arises when the projective meaning of the world has already been crippled by the fixed intellectual stare we discussed earlier. Only when things have lost their practical everyday interrelatedness and have taken on the character of mere things filling up space with fixed properties and attributes does the question of meaninglessness arise. But this is not the primordial state of the world; it is rather a degenerate form of the ordinary, meaningful understanding of things in a world.

But, again, we are getting ahead of our story. The task of exposing the traditional view of meaning as the source of meaninglessness belongs to the next chapter.

[53] *Ibid.*

CHAPTER 3

MEANING AND MEANINGLESSNESS

This brings us to the central thesis of the book, the claim that meaninglessness is based on the traditional concept of meaning, the irony that the search for meaning has led and must lead to a sense of meaninglessness. In the previous chapter we saw that what opposes the recognition of projection or being-as is the objectivist view of reality. However refined in its philosophical articulation, the root of the idea is the naive realist position of common sense, that things *are* just as they *appear*, that the true interpretation is simply part of the thing itself and somehow identical with it, i.e., its real nature or essence. Thus, recognition that any comprehensible aspect of a thing is a human interpretation from a particular standpoint, and that all intelligible meaning is therefore projection, is a tacit denial of the objectivist view of meaning, and this leads to a sense of meaninglessness.

Meaninglessness, we have said, is an awareness that meaning is projection, but this awareness rests on a nonprojective interpretation of meaning. Meaninglessness is the recognition that meaning is projection, but only in the sense in which this implies that meaning is *not nonprojection*, i.e., that it is *not* the real nature of the thing itself as we have previously supposed. It is a *denial* of the naive objectivist view of meaning and reality, the perceived *contrast* between the fact that meaning is projection and the traditional ideal of a nonprojective meaning identical with, or at least not distinguished from, the thing itself. The tragic sense of meaninglessness is therefore like a rich man who has lost all his money. *His* tragedy, as Aristotle saw, implies a *fall*; unlike the usual sort of dissatisfaction in not having enough money, *his* sense of poverty presupposes his first having been *rich*.

The search for the true meaning of X has traditionally been conceived as eliminating all subjectively oriented interpretations in order to get down to the real nature of the thing itself. But, like peeling the layers of an onion, this only succeeds in drawing our attention to the projective nature of meaning, and hence the falsity of the non-projective ideal, the result of which is a sense of meaninglessness.

Thus, while projection is the source of meaning, the awareness of projection is the source of meaninglessness. Meaning *is* (in fact) projection, we may say, but it is normally *perceived* as nonprojection. When we analyse meaning we find that it rests on projection, but since this clashes with the deep-seated nonprojective ideal of meaning, it is tantamount to saying that things are meaningless. Since the search for meaning reveals projection, the search for meaning (in the traditional, nonprojection sense) leads to meaninglessness. Dialectically, the realist theory of meaning eventually destroys itself.

In this chapter we want to see exactly how this happens, starting from the most obvious common sense descriptive level and working our way through to the more difficult philosophical analysis of this complex phenomenon. Thus, we will circle round the problem in a narrowing spiral, gradually clarifying and making more articulate our analysis as we move progressively inward toward the philosophical center of the problem.

On the most mundane level, we have already mentioned how meaninglessness inevitably appears as the intentional object of the absolutist standpoint, the point of view of "what will it matter 5000 years from now." When we seek an "objective," realistic view, we try to remove all personal, historical or cultural biases and take the long-range view. But what we discover from this absolutist perspective is that things suddenly become pointless and absurd. In general, any disengaged or unengaged point of view tends to reveal the senseless absurdity of things. In everyday life, through habit, training or inclination, our interests are engaged in certain activities and disengaged from others, and those from which we are disengaged will inevitably seem more pointless and absurd. Traditionally, to search for meaning is to try to disengage from any human point of view, and this leads to meaninglessness.

Beginning philosophy students, for example, often suffer from misology. Observing from a detached distance the historical rise and fall of different philosophies, each confidently asserting itself and denying all the others, each nevertheless destined to be eventually refuted or forgotten, they wonder "what is the point of doing philo-sophy?" And from *this* point of view, the answer is "None." That it all seems quite pointless is the natural expression of an aloof attitude standing back, looking down on the history of thought. To the beginning student it seems utterly pointless to engage in yet another dreary philosophical debate for this or that current ism against some other. That people can get "worked up" about this sort of thing is more an object for wonder than of serious concern. But it does not, or at least not always, appear so absurd to the aca-demic philosopher. Why not? Ironically, because he takes a less "philosophic" stance. He does not, at least normally, see it "object-ively" from the perspective of 5000 years hence. He happens to be involved here and now in the current debate, he is himself caught up in the thick of things, and from *this* perspective it *is* meaningful.

Our philosopher, let us say, is an Austrian studying science at the University of Vienna in the 1920's. He feels that his generation will turn the tide of intellectual history from the dark alleyways of super-stition and obscurity to the positive light of scientific method. He is an architect of a brave new world, and he identifies and defines himself in terms of this struggle. Or perhaps, he becomes disillusioned with the dehumanizing effect of this brave new world and throws in his lot with the existentialist defenders of the religious or humanistic faith. In either case it is his complete immersion in the immediate milieu which gives his work meaning. 5000 years later, or perhaps only 50, it will be difficult to take any of this seriously, but at the time it has a meaningful look.

The objection to the supposed meaninglessness of things *sub specie aeternatatis* is simply that we live here and now, not elsewhere or nowhere 5000 years hence. It is not that the absolutist point of view is wrong, but that it has no greater claim to truth than the engaged point of view of the concerned person. We can agree with the *ultimate* senselessness of things *sub specie aeternatatis*, but, aside from a certain metaphysical nostalgia for permanence and a sense of world weariness, there is no reason to prefer this ultimate point of view to some more immediate perspective.

In this sense radical hippies, like Charles Manson, appear to have swallowed a dangerous half-truth. *Ultimately*, the individual is only part of a much larger natural order and his death is consequently unimportant or even unreal, but *here and now* the man's life is obviously very precious to him. *Both* points of view are important and must be taken into account. *Sub specie aeternatatis* all is pointless and absurd, including the writing of philosophy, even philosophy *sub specie aeternatatis*. Why then, we might ask, does the philosopher of the absolutist standpoint bother putting pen to paper? Because, like the rest of us, he does not live only and always within the absolutist perspective. He, too, is caught up in the more immediate day to day concerns of attracting and instructing disciples, gaining fame, overcoming hostile critics, turning his people back to the path of reason and righteousness, etc., and this projects meaning and importance into what is, from the absolutist point of view, a thoroughly meaningless occupation.

To the mystic there is little point in following the hourly news broadcast, which may be highly significant for the guerilla fighter; to the scientifically trained engineer the most exciting and "meaningful" new theological talk may seen quite a pathetic and futile opposition to the inevitable and desirable decline of religion. Neither point of view has any absolute priority over the other, and in daily life we find ourselves, in different situations, adopting both. If we lived always and only in the absolutist perspective, things just *would be* pointless; and if we were constantly engaged in some immediate point of view, meaninglessness could never enter our experience. But we don't do either exclusively; both points of view are available to the plain man in the everyday context. One moment an overheard conversation sounds senseless and stupid; but the next moment we have entered into the conversation and the same ultimately pointless trivialities engage our interest and take on considerable meaning. One day we scoff at the petty absurdity of office or academic politics, but later we are drawn into the fray and it all seems terribly important and interesting. We can draw close to events and project meaning, or we can withdraw and observe that façade of meaning disappear.

Consider, for example, Macbeth's world-weary soliloquy,

Tomorrow, and tomorrow, and tomorrow,
Creeps in this petty pace from day to day,
To the last syllable of recorded time;
And all our yesterdays have lighted fools
The way to dusty death. Out, out brief candle!
Life's but a walking shadow; a poor player,
That struts and frets his hour upon the stage,
And then is no more; it is a tale

Told by an idiot, full of sound and fury,
Signifying nothing.[1]

This disconnected, end-of-the-line perspective is obviously very
different from Macbeth's earlier robust plunge into the turmoil
of harsh political realities. Or, compare Antoine's aloof attitude
toward the cafe lovers in *Nausea* with the involved attitude of the
lovers themselves.

They find the world pleasant as it is, just as it is, and each one of them,
temporarily, draws life from the life of the other. Soon the two of them
will make a single life, a slow, tepid life which will have no sense at all—but
they won't notice it.[2]

To the lovers their affair is of the utmost significance and importance,
highly charged with meaning. But Antoine, who is detached from
them, and from love and life in general, sees it as just one more human
coupling since time began. This does not mean that the couples are
blind or that Antoine is a fool; it is just that in ordinary circumstances
we can and do see the world in both ways. The world will yield up
either aspect, and the point for our present analysis is that the attempt
to block projection by eliminating subjective, historical, cultural
biases does not reveal the true meaning or the real nature of the
objective thing itself, but simply meaninglessness. Because the search
for meaning in the traditional objectivist sense implies the elimination
of subjective biases and points of view, the search for meaning in the
traditional sense always leads to meaninglessness.

In a more general way, our awareness of different points of view,
and the attempt to choose the "right" one and to gradually improve
on it, can lead to a sense of relativism, and from there to an awareness
of projection and meaninglessness. The discarded, subjectively-biased
view gently mocks us with the question, "And why not the present
one?" the implications of which, like one's fifth or sixth marriage,
become more persuasive the longer the series. Our awareness of
shifts of aspect, of the historical development of ideas and of our
own evolving points of view, when judged from the naive realist
standpoint of objective meaning, can lead to a sense of meaninglessness. Searching for objective meaning we discover meaninglessness.

---

[1] Shakespeare, William, *Macbeth*, in: *The Complete Works of Shakespeare*
(George L. Kittredge, ed.), Boston: Ginn and Company, 1936, p. 1142.

[2] Sartre, Jean-Paul, *Nausea* (Lloyd Alexander, trans.), Norfolk, Connecticut:
New Directions Books, 1959, p. 145.

Closer to the philosophical problem is the rise of science and the consequent "neutralization of nature," [3] which we suggested in the last chapter is really part of a much larger attempt to eliminate projection. Given the reality criterion of Being discussed earlier, the search for truth and meaning becomes the attempt to eliminate all forms of subjective bias. We naturally react first to the most obvious forms of human projection, retaining the rest; then, moving on to less obvious cases, we press our attack home until hopefully we arrive at the real, objective nature of things. In fact, this only leads to meaninglessness. It is this anti-projection, objectivist position which helps explain the rise of early Greek philosophy, as well as the New Science and Enlightenment which followed later. In fact the entire history of Western thought (both philosophical and scientific) can be seen as a retreat from meaning in the hope of finding reality. In a sense this has been achieved, though not in the way expected. The reality so discovered has turned out woefully short of any intelligible meaning, and the result has been a sense of meaninglessness.

Of course, this has happened only gradually. Each successive retreat from meaning is an adjustment to a world more neutral and sterile than its predecessor. But at least in the past some adjustment has always been possible simply by attaching greater importance to whatever remained of projected meaning. If concrete perceptual elements were discarded, then the sublime beauty of abstractions was praised. If teleology was found incompatible with reality, then the perfect clockwork regularity of the universe was admired. If emotion was thought to be a projected façade, then the regard for reason and intellect went up appreciably. If the universe could no longer be seen as controlled by intelligible laws, then man's control over nature through statistical regularities was glorified. And so on. At each stage some residue remained with which men could identify at least a part of themselves.

Thus, we can reconstruct the history of ideas from pre-philosophic cosmologies, to the more intellectually abstract early Greek and Scholastic philosophy and science, to the secular and humanistic enlightenment, to the mechanistic new science, to the particularist control-oriented probabilities of current scientific thinking. Generally,

---

[3] Richards, I. A., *Science and Poetry*, in: *A Modern Book of Esthetics* (Melvin Rader, ed.), Holt, Rinehart and Winston, Inc., 1960, p. 272.

that is, up to the present the shift has always been in favor of reason and intellect at the expense of perception, emotion and volition. But in the most recent period even reason has been sacrificed to reality, and we are left with control and raw (i.e., disconnected, meaningless) power. This can be very clearly observed, for example, in the changing fashion in regard to permissible forms of explanation. Teleological explanations, in many ways the most thorough and satisfying, gave way to formal or essentialist explanations in terms of the real nature of X. This was attacked by Bacon and others as the projection of merely linguistic concerns, and essentialist explanations gradually receded before the advance of mechanical causes and Natural Law, themselves, eventually to be overtaken by mathematical, non-mechanical explanations. But even this satisfied the desire to perceive a rational order in nature, a desire which has now, apparently, given place to control-oriented statistical averages, the lower limit of explanation, scarcely counting as such. Explanation is generally understood to provide a frame of reference in terms of which we perceive some part of reality, and this means that we project some part of ourselves into the explanation, seeing phenomena as obeying laws, pursuing a goal, the product of rational design, and so on. By elimination projection, we have been led to construct scientific hypotheses which no longer satisfy the original demand for explanation. We no longer *understand* the world in terms of our explanations, we simply *use* them to control the environment. Explanations now satisfy only the desire for power and control.

Not that everyone wholeheartedly embraced each new departure from meaning. At each stage there was a strong reaction. Socrates' contemporaries saw a threat to religion, as did the critics of Galileo and Newton. Leibniz and the later Scholastics saw a threat to moral reason and teleology. The Romantics saw a threat to the emotional physiognomy of nature, and the early Existentialists have agonized over the loss of man's individuality and freedom in a reason-dominated universe, while the later Existentialists express anxiety over the infinite freedom of man in the irrational world of Indeterminacy. But to the most recent exposure of subjective bias in the last vestige of rationality and order the response has been an increasing sense of nihilism, expressed as anarchy, violence, psychosis and alienation. The history of intellectual thought from the Middle Ages to the present is one of the ever decreasing limits of reason in the sense of seeing man's place in nature and the ever increasing scope of manipulative reason to order man's life and control nature. When the neutralization of nature is complete, what is left but the idea of control and power? But power over what? For what? No one can say, just more and more power, power for power's sake, i.e., for the sake of nothing.

The response has been a sense of alienation and meaninglessness. We find ourselves thrown up on a shore of alien, incomprehensible and therefore oppressive and stifling matter. Cut off from a meaningful world, language becomes senseless, mechanical; genuine emotional response becomes impossible. As Rilke saw, the coherence of the internal world depends on a meaningful relation to an interpreted external world [4] (what Eliot called the "objective correlative"). [5] Without the one, the other shrivels and dies.

But this very meaninglessness arises directly out of the firm conviction that the world does have a meaning, that however obscured by layers of subjective bias and cultural prejudice, the real meaning can be extracted from the interpreted world and perceived as it actually is. The desire to strip away the layers of meaning, which leads to meaninglessness, is nourished by this belief in a hard core of objective meaning beneath the layers. The sense of meaninglessness rests squarely on the concept of meaning.

An interesting example of meaninglessness arising out of the traditional, realist conception of meaning is the outcome of the Romantic tension regarding aesthetic imagination. The vacillation discernible in Romantic theories of poetry is due primarily to an ambivalent attitude towards the objectivity of poetic or "secondary" imagination. Unable to reconcile the idea that aesthetics should form part of the perceptible, public universe with the fact that perceiving it as such is a form of projection, Romantic writers like Coleridge and Wordsworth vacillated uneasily between the idea that aesthetic imagination was an alternative, equally objective way of apprehending the world and the idea that it merely shed a beautiful but false light on an objective, nonaesthetic reality. Unable to rid themselves entirely of the realist criterion of meaning, they identified aesthetic perception with projection, projection with distortion, and thus drifted progressively toward pessimism, meaninglessness and an

---

[4] Rilke, Rainer Maria, *Duino Elegies* (J. B. Leishman and Stephen Spender, trans.), London: The Hogarth Press, 1939.

[5] Eliot, T. S., "Hamlet," in: *Elizabethan Essays*, New York: Haskell House, 1964, p. 61.

other-worldly spiritualism. An examination of the conditions of poetic meaning thus revealed an aesthetically and emotionally meaningless world.

Does poetry *discover* the "one interior life/That lives in all things," [6] "the positive principle of life ... spread through the entire creation," [7] or is it rather that poetry "*puts* a spirit of life and motion *into* the universe," [8] as suggested by Romantic terminology (overflow, *ausdruck*, express, endow, pourforth, vent)? Wordsworth and Coleridge couldn't decide. The ambiguity in their accounts of poetic imagination is traceable to the ambiguity in key concepts like "transformation." Does this mean to *correct* the distorted scientific picture of reality or to *distort* for beauty's sake the real nature of things? The Romantics were unable to give any decisive answer, drifting uneasily between these alternatives, settling finally on the aesthetically nihilistic distortion interpretation. If Wordsworth and Schelling drift toward spiritualism and pessimism, it is only because they cannot let go the realist theory of meaning, that any form of projection is a distortion of the real (in this case, Newtonian) nature of reality. Again, the search for meaning has led to meaninglessness.

Ironically, even the attempt to shore up a dwindling sense of meaningfulness by recourse to a transcendent source and guarantee of meaning (God, Platonic Ideas, the Absolute, spiritualism) has had just the opposite effect of increasing the sense of meaninglessness. On the one hand, these transcendent guarantors of meaning are required by the commonsense and philosophic realist view of "objective" meaning, and on the other hand, they represent a retreat from a meaningful world of everyday experience. The realist criterion of meaning requires an underlying core of meaning only loosely manifested in the confusing world of ordinary appearance, thus tending to transfer the ordinary meaning of "appearances" to the "real" source of meaning, and *implicitly*, giving up meaning in the everyday sphere.

---

[6] Wordsworth, William, *The Prelude*, Book II (MS RV, not in the published text), in: *The Prelude* (edited by Ernest De Selincourt and revised by Helen Darbishire), Oxford: Clarendon Press, 1959, p. 525. Cf. published text 1805, "... for in all things/I saw one life ...", *Ibid.*, p. 66).

[7] Schelling, F. W. J., *Von der Weltseele*, in: *Schellings Werke*, vol. I, Leipzig, 1907, p. 599.

[8] Hazlitt, William. "On Poetry in General", in *Selected Essays af William Hazlitt* (Geoffrey Keynes, ed.). New York: Random House, 1930, p. 389.

Then as this everyday world begins to lose what meaning it had, especially during periods of religious, philosophic or scientific upheaval, the transcendent source of meaning is more heavily relied upon to stem the tide and preserve meaning. This conservative influence is evident, for example, in Plato, Santayana, Whitehead, and the late Romantics, where the real meaning of the world, hidden from the casual observer, is held to be permanent, unchanging and hence transcendent, whether God, Idea, the Absolute or the immutable Laws of Nature. As the everyday world becomes more meaningless and alien, we turn increasingly to this transcendent source. But as we do, we are giving over more and more meaning to this transcendent source at the expense of the interrelated significance of things in the everyday world. Implicitly, we have already lost the sense of this everyday meaningfullness; we see it now only derivatively as a pale reflection of God, Law or Order. But the realist criterion of meaning is no special friend of religion; as soon as we realize that this too is projection, then all is lost. Nothing is left.

Basically the same problem confronts any form of transcendentalism, whether religious, philosophical or scientific. The natural heir to the naive realist sense of meaning, and its second line of defense, is that the ordinary world of appearances hides a deeper reality which is precisely what the ordinary world of appearances ought to be but is not—identical in essence and existence, being and meaning. If the ordinary world of everyday experience turns out to be projection, then there must be some other, second-order reality "beneath" or "underlying" this one which is truly nonprojective—whether the mechanical reality of Newtonian physics, the unchanging nature of God or the self-identity of philosophical substance. When this second line of defense gives way, either through anthropological accounts of the idea of God, the ultimate unintelligibility of the nature of substance (which we shall discuss in a moment), or the Indeterminacy-Relativity shock to the scientific transcendentalism of traditional mechanics, there is nothing left but meaninglessness.

Thus far we have been discussing the natural historical and cultural drift toward meaninglessness. Now we want to see how the explicitly philosophical search into conditions of truth and meaning has led directly to the modern experience of meaninglessness. Narrowing our spiral by another turn, we begin with the interesting and instructive contradictions in Nietzsche's theory of truth. Nietzsche saw that a thoroughly honest exploration into the conditions of cognition revealed that knowledge was based unalterably on projection, from which he concluded that knowledge was a meaningless illusion. This is obviously contradictory. If it's knowledge, it's not illusory; if it's illusory, it's not knowledge. The theory assumes that truth is both projection and nonprojection. On the one hand, the conclusion states that knowledge *is* projection; on the other hand, it asserts that our so-called knowledge is a meaningless illusion, and this implies that real knowledge is *not* projection. But how can the source of knowledge, projection, be the source of our lack of knowledge? Only if projection is unfavorably contrasted with our traditional concept of knowledge, only if the argument rests on the nonprojective, realist theory of meaning and truth. Why is knowledge illusory on Nietzsche's view? Because it is based on projection. But what is illusory about projection. Its subjective orientation. But what's wrong with that? Simply that knowledge by definition must correspond directly with objective reality, admitting no gap between thought and the object of thought. In other words, the projective nature of knowledge is illusory because knowledge must be nonprojective.

For Nietzsche truth, or what we *call* truth, is a form of deception necessary for life. What he had in mind most probably was a recognition of the subjective orientation necessary to perceive or know anything, hence projection as a necessary condition for truth. In this sense Nietzsche denied the correspondence, or realist theory of truth, that truth simply mirrors the real nature of things. But it does not follow from this that what we call truth is a form of deception. Indeed, to say that truth is deception implies that it does *not* mirror reality. Why *should* it mirror reality, except on terms dictated by the deposed realist or correspondence sense of truth? Hence the contradiction, or at least vacillation, in Nietzsche's account. On the one hand there *is* truth, but it is a pragmatic rather than a correspondence truth. But this means there is no correspondence truth. And if there's no correspondence truth, then what we *call* truth, i.e., pragmatic truth, is nothing but a sham. It is like saying that the physical world is ugly because there are no objective aesthetic values or, less decorously, that a man is naked because his clothes are unfashionable. To be consistent Nietzsche should have said either that the criterion of truth was correspondence and there *was* no truth (i.e., no instances of the concept), or that the criterion of truth was pragmatic and there *was* truth (i.e., instances of the concept). But to say both, that there is no truth because truth is pragmatic, is contradictory. But the contradiction is instructive because it illustrates the deep-seated tenacity of the realist criterion of truth and meaning.

The difficulty Nietzsche faces, of course, is in trying to redefine a concept with a long-accepted usage. Confusions of this sort are analyzable into two factors, the concept and those things commonly classified under that concept. Since the word refers indifferently to both, there is room for confusion, and the confusion comes to a head if the character of the instances contradicts the terms by which the concept is defined, that is, if the instances do not deserve to be so classified. "Research scholar," for example, refers to either a person engaged in scholarly research or to someone who is paid to do so. It is possible that a person who is paid to do scholarly research actually spends his time drinking coffee and playing squash, but to describe this situation will prove very ticklish. We may say that there is no (real) research scholar here at all, meaning no one who meets the criteria, or we may say that this "research scholar" is not (really) a research scholar, meaning that even though he is so paid he doesn't meet the criteria, but whatever we say has a ring of irony or contradiction. If we become philosophical and try to redefine "research scholar" in terms of the "facts," the confusion deepens hopelessly. "To be a research scholar is neither to be a scholar nor to do research." But notice that the confusion depends on retaining the original concept. Similarly, for any reductive analysis. "Justice is nothing but the interest of the stronger. Therefore there *is* no real justice in the world today." Why? (After all, there surely *are* strong men who get what they want.) Because action in the interests of the stronger is unjust! Here, too, the confusion arises out of both denying and also retaining the original concept. It is a failure to recognize the difference between denying *instances* of a concept and denying the standard *meaning* of that concept.

So in Nietzsche's case, the problem depends on the fact that the whole discussion takes place within the framework of the realist criterion of meaning and truth. Nietzsche first addresses himself to the correspondence criterion of truth and discovers there is nothing answering to this. But instead of concluding that there is no truth, he tries to redefine what actually goes by that name, thus setting up a new criterion of truth (social and biological utility). According to *this* criterion there is and must be truth. But Nietzsche doesn't stop here; reintroducing the deposed realist criterion, he decries the deceptiveness of truth, from which we can only escape, ironically enough, through a different, but more pleasant, form of deception, namely, art.

Had we not approved the arts and invented this kind of cult of the untrue, then the insight into the universal untruth and mendacity, which is now given to us by science—the insight into delusion and error as conditions of cognition and sentient experience—would not be endurable at all. Honesty would have disgust and suicide in its train. But now our honesty has an opposing force which helps us to avoid such consequences; art, as the *good* will to appearance.[9]

And what of reality on Nietzsche's view? With the same kind of contradictory reasoning he argues that since reality can never be known in itself, it must be random and unintelligible. But again, this only makes sense, if it makes sense at all, in terms of the realist criterion of truth and meaning. If intelligibility, and orderly scientific truth are projections, then, according to the realist criterion, the thing itself must be *un*intelligible, *dis*orderly, and meaningless. Without this assumed criterion, the conclusion would not follow at all; all that would follow is that to know the thing in itself in the realist sense is logically impossible.

The point is, to search for the conditions of truth, is to discover the human factor (projection), and because of the realist criterion, this means that science is deceptive and the world unintelligible and meaningless. Insofar as the realist conception of meaning and truth always invites this candid scrutiny, it is inherently unstable, dialectically tending always to undermine itself. The search for meaning leads to meaninglessness.

Similarly, language philosophers like Korzybski argue that since there is no meaning which cannot be expressed linguistically and no linguistic expression without subjectively biased concepts and forms of thought, all thought and language must be a distortion of reality.[10] These philosophers argue quite rightly that words are not to be confused with objects, that language is a human tool for illuminating certain aspects of the world without which there could be no meaningful world at all. That is, they have recognized that meaning is

[9] Nietzsche, Friedrich, *The Will to Power* (A. M. Ludovici, trans.), in: *The Complete Works of Friedrich Nietzsche* (Oscar Levy, ed.), vol. 15, New York: Russell and Russell, 1964, pp. 291-292.

[10] Korzybski, Alfred, *Science and Sanity*, New York: The International non-Aristotelian Library Publishing Co., 1941.

projection and that the realist theory is naive and false. But they conclude from this that language (and thought) *distort* or *falsify* reality. Why? Because it is *not* identical with the object, because it does not just state the real essence of the thing as it is in itself. But what would lead one to suppose that knowledge *ought* to be congruent with the object? Nothing less than the realist theory supposedly being denied! Thus in one breath the realist criterion of meaning is discarded as naive while in the very next breath it is reintroduced and used to condemn our convention-bound thought and language. The realist criterion invites a search into the subjective conditions of meaning and this leads to a sense of meaninglessness.

How is meaning possible? Because we have developed concepts and articulated points of view. But this implies that meaning is limited to a human frame of reference and is therefore projection. But if it is subjectively biased, then it distorts our view of the real nature of things. Our concepts get in the way of a true grasp of reality, yet we can't think at all without this subjective veil. And so we feel trapped in an illusion from which there is no escape. Whatever we think is false, the world as we experience it is ultimately meaningless. At the persuasive heart of this reasoning is the nonprojective ideal of meaning.

The attempt to simply analyse the conditions of truth and meaning *without* reference to the nonprojective, realist criterion is the basis of the phenomenological movement, at least in its early phase. In the "natural attitude" our thought is directed toward objects perceived as just given in cognition. "Just" means that there is no awareness of projection, or any recognized gap between the object and how I see it, or if there is a gap it is seen as the source of error and falsehood. The natural attitude is naive in that it does not take into account *how* our thought is directed at the object; it is only concerned with the object itself. This is the context in which traditional epistemology and metaphysics arise and without which they would be unintelligible. As Husserl says,

The natural attitude of mind ... is as yet unconcerned with the critique of cognition ... . In the natural mode of reflection we are turned to *the objects* as they are given to us each time ... . In perception, for instance, a thing stands before our eyes as a matter of course.[11]

---

[11] Husserl, Edmund, *The Idea of Phenomenology* (William Alston and George Nakhnikian, trans.), The Hague: Martinus Nijhoff, 1964, p. 13

One of the main reasons for Husserl's analysis of the natural attitude is to show that however much epistemologists and metaphysicians have sought to disparage and deny the commonsense outlook, all their efforts take place entirely within this commonsense framework and would be unintelligible without it, and that until we understand this, we cannot understand what traditional philosophers have really been up to and why they have failed.

To illustrate this point I want to consider several examples from traditional philosophy. The first is the familiar tale, already mentioned in the previous chapter, of scepticism in regard to the senses and the arguments for the existence of sense data. In going over all this again I only want to stress the point which I think is generally neglected, that these arguments presuppose, and make no sense without, the realist criterion of meaning. The sceptic argues that what we perceive is not identical with what we claim or know the object to be, and that therefore we don't really *see* the object. He says that since we don't see all of it, or every side and aspect of it, and since what we do see is from a limited perspective, we cannot be said to perceive the object as we had supposed. He is contrasting, in other words, the actual conditions of perception with the *a priori* concept or criterion of perception. And what can this *a priori* criterion be but the realist criterion that to see X is to see all of it just as it is in itself. Now where does this assumption come from? Ordinary-language philosophers, like Austin, suggest that it is a fabrication of the epistemologist. But this overlooks the fact that the argument is addressed to and found persuasive by the plain man. It is the plain man who is ready to admit that if there is a gap between the object and his perception of it, then he doesn't really see it. That there *is* such a gap in ordinary perception the sceptic must demonstrate to the plain man, but that such a gap contradicts the concept of perception is already an assumption of ordinary language and common sense. This is the one point on which the philosopher and the plain man agree, and it is Austin who is odd man out. Without this assumption the argument falls quite flat, losing that *prima facie* appeal which it undoubtedly has.

Let's drop the assumption for a moment and see what happens. When the traditional philosopher points out that we can't see all of the object at the same time, that we can never get a complete view which coincides with the real nature of the thing itself, we would reply that, while this was so, it does not prove that we can't really see the object, because (borrowing a line from the ordinary-language philosophers) "seeing" just *means* getting a partial glimpse of the thing from a particular angle. To show our cleverness, we might add that if the object is opaque, it would be ridiculous to suppose that perception could be anything else. But now the whole point of the argument has been lost. "Seeing" *doesn't* just mean getting a partial glimpse from a limited standpoint; it also and primarily means seeing the whole thing, completely, just as it is. Thus the dilemma indicated by the sense datum philosophers is, implicitly, potentially, the dilemma of common sense, and the ambiguity of "see" is the ambiguity of ordinary language. The basis of the argument is the firm belief, or assumption of the man-in-the-street that subjective biases must not get in the way of perception and cognition and that, when they do, they distort our view of things. All the sceptic does is to show, and rightly so, that perception without subjective bias is impossible. The argument has the effect, in the long run a useful effect, of making us less naive regarding our knowledge of the external world. We begin to understand the subjective conditions necessary for knowledge. Unfortunately, though, we haven't yet dropped the old ideal, and so the argument does its work by bringing us face-to-face with the irreconcilable conflict between our objective *idea* of perception and the actual subjective conditions necessary to it. The conclusion to the argument *ought* to be that *one* of these conflicting positions must be false: either knowledge is *not* incompatible with the gap between the object and our perception of it or there is *not* such a gap. Most critics of scepticism, themselves deeply sunk in the realist criterion of meaning, have opted for the latter, looking for a form of perception (the sensing of sense data) which does meet the realist criterion. But this is logically inconsistent as we have seen. Whatever is to count as perception must involve some element of human interpretation. The solution, or dissolution, therefore, lies in attacking the first position, that is, the realist criterion itself, though this is a much more difficult task than philosophers up to now have been willing to consider. (Of course, you do not attack the realist criterion simply by denying its existence, as the ordinary-language philosophers have done.)

Again, the point I wish to emphasize is that the search for meaning leads to meaninglessness. The harder we try to discover what we really perceive, the more we are led to the conclusion that we really perceive nothing.

Our second example concerns certain metaphysical difficulties over the concept, substance. Seventeenth century philosophers followed the common-sense assumptions contained in the venerable doctrine of substance into a beautiful *cul de sac*. Again, the motive was to eliminate projection and interpretation in order to discover what the thing itself is really like. Following common sense and ordinary language, philosophers have always distinguished the properties of a thing from that thing itself. What Locke and others discovered was that the properties of a thing were always and necessarily what we *understood* or *thought* about the thing. In each case properties turned out to be interpretations and therefore subjectively oriented, if not located. And vice versa, whatever was thought or said about the thing was understood as a property of it. This raised an interesting problem. What then *was* the thing itself? What could we know of it? Apparently, nothing. Whatever was put forward as a candidate for knowledge of the thing itself must be a description capable of being thought and expressed in language, and this meant that it was a property attributed *to*, or said *of*, the thing itself but *not* that thing itself. The thing itself became an embarrassingly obscure I-know-not-what. Again, the search for meaning was understood as the elimination of projection, and this led to the recognition of the extent of projection and hence to meaninglessness.

A final example is the philosopher's worry over antinomies, two contradictory statements both of which appear equally supported by reason. Consider the antinomy derived from the mind-body problem. The thesis states that mind and body can't interact; the anti-thesis states that they must interact. Both are supported by reason. Mind is not physical; it has no spatial extension or mechanical movement or power; therefore it can't touch, or be touched, by a body which is a necessary condition for interaction. On the other hand, feeling pain from a cut foot, or carrying out a decision to raise my arm clearly presupposes interaction. How have philosophers got themselves into this dilemma? The reason, I suggest, is the objectivist view of meaning; i.e., they have taken their own talk too literally, assuming a direct and objective correspondence between words and objects. In ordinary speech we do talk of minds and bodies and we do draw some sort of distinction between them. We say she has a fine body but a weak mind, we encourage sound minds in sound bodies, or we complain that the spirit is willing but the flesh is weak, and vice versa. But this is just a way of speaking; we don't mean that there are two distinct classes of objects, minds and bodies.

The philosopher insists that this is nonetheless *implied* in our ordinary language, and he tries to hold us to the logical implications of this otherwise convenient and frequently illuminating ordinary way of speaking. He insists that if we are to speak seriously, we must speak strictly and literally; thus, if mind and body are distinct, then they are utterly distinct, literally cut off from one another. He thus takes our ordinary distinction and makes something of it. It is *our* distinction but we hardly recognize it when he has finished working out its logical implications and tightening it up. What the traditional philosopher has failed to see is that words don't relate to the world in this simple mechanical correspondence fashion. But why does the philosopher insist on this correspondence metaphor? Because he wants to get at the real meaning, the real objective nature of things. For this reason, loose, casual ways of speaking are just not good enough. He demands that we say what we mean and mean what we say. Why? To insure that our thoughts mirror reality. The root of his thinking and the drive behind it is the realist criterion of meaning.

How do we solve these antinomies? By distinguishing two kinds of distinction, a convenient, conventional, ordinary distinction which we will allow, and an absolute, literal, philosophical distinction whose use we must censure. Is mind distinct from body? This and similar questions should be answered boldly with a firm and decisive "yes and no." In the sense in which we find it useful to speak of people in these two rather different ways, yes. In the sense in which "mind" and "body" literally denote two entities in the world absolutely distinct from one another, no. Are properties different from things? Again, yes and no. In the sense in which we find it convenient to refer various descriptions and pieces of information to some common focal point, yes. But in the sense in which this way of speaking is taken to mean that objects in the world fall into two distinct kinds, properties and things, no. In ordinary speech, for example, it would never occur to us to discuss the thing without its properties. It is only when we forget the projective, vonventional nature of language and expect language to literally mirror or duplicate the world that we begin to make this sort of supposition.

Behind all these philosophical difficulties lies the realist criterion of meaning, the backbone both of common sense and, in a more sophisticated form, traditional philosophy. The realist criterion of meaning demands that meaning be identical with the thing itself. This is the view of ordinary experience. But at the first whiff of projection, the mind becomes critical, adopting a "search and destroy" attitude toward all forms of projection, with the hope of eventually discovering the hard core of nonprojected meaning underlying the deceitful world of ordinary appearances. But the critical attitude knows no bounds; once this hard core of nonprojective meaning is seen to be infected with the same rot of projection, the only conclusion to be drawn is that the world is thoroughly meaningless. Once this process has begun there seems no way to reverse or resist its inevitable conclusion.

This dialectical tension between meaning and meaninglessness springing from the realist criterion is nowhere so clearly set forth as in Heidegger. Ironically, Heidegger's analysis is both the most philosophically profound and the most mundane; it is the clearest philosophical statement of the tension of meaning *within ordinary experience*. Failure to appreciate this point has led to a serious misunderstanding of Heidegger. His analysis is often difficult and obscure, but what he is analyzing is always something right under our nose. Far more than Moore and the Scottish philosophers, Heidegger is the philosopher of common sense *par excellence*.

Man's way of being is to understand Being; or, as we have been saying, it is man's nature to project meaning. But projection is essentially blind; it conceals our responsibility for the intelligible meaning, or being-as of the world, luring us out of ourselves into a "real world" of substantial "things." This leads to the realist, anti-projection criterion of meaning, which, when applied philosophically, scientifically, leads to an awareness of the nature and extent of projection and hence to meaninglessness. What Heidegger's analysis shows is that, quite apart from any philosophic reflection, meaninglessness is a necessary feature of *ordinary experience*; the dialectical tension between meaning and meaninglessness he presents as an analysis of ordinary human existence. And so, our spiral winds down another notch.

It is man's nature to project meaning, and to be successful this must be a blind, naive throwing of ourselves into things. Thus, projecting meaning, having a meaningful world, leads to a forgetfulness of projection and thus a forgetfulness of ourselves as projecting meaning. But absolute self-opaqueness is more characteristic of animal existence than of human nature. What prevents a *complete* forgetfulness of being-as and of ourselves as responsible for being-as is the fear of losing ourselves in external objects. This, then, tends towards an awareness of ourselves as projecting meaning. But neither is perfect self-knowledge characteristic of ordinary human experience; what prevents *its* full expression is the fear of meaninglessness. The two extremes tend to opposite directions, yet ironically both lead to the same conclusion—meaninglessness. To the extent that we become aware of ourselves as projecting meaning we are made to see that things in themselves are nothing, that it is we who are responsible for the meaning of the world. But we dread this realization and react by becoming more absorbed in things. To the extent that we are lost in an external world we are alienated from ourselves, with the same result, a sense of an absurd, meaningless world. The net result is a dull anxiety or uneasiness; not quite absorbed in projected meanings, vaguely aware of ourselves as projecting, tending now toward the one, now toward the other—a state best described as trying to forget, or run away from, something.

Thus, Heidegger analyzes ordinary human experience as the product of two opposing forces, both of which are constantly present in varying degrees, creating a fragile tension. Insofar as we project meaning, we tend to lose ourselves in things. But this makes us anxious for our self-identity. But insofar as we accept our projecting nature we are brought to a sense of meaninglessness, the only escape from which is to blindly project meaning.

The analysis is dialectical, like the description of a moving pendulum; once a certain point is reached, the equal and opposite reaction sets in, the extreme point of which is met by an opposite reaction back to the original position. This is not a temporal analysis, but an analysis of dynamic forces omnipresent in experience. At any given moment, according to Heidegger, both forces are at work and the net result is a sense of uneasiness, a guilty pretense, which Sartre calls "bad faith." We can't quite face ourselves and we can't quite lose ourselves, and so we are stuck in between balancing on a tight-rope drawn between the two extremes. Because the factors are opposed, a temporal movement *can* be established between the two poles as a secondary phenomenon, and to that extent Heidegger's analysis has been used to explore the progression of various stages within human experience. But neither extreme is ever fully reached, and the whole point of the pendulum or dialectic concept is that the reactive forces are powerfully present at all times. As the pendulum reaches the fartherest point to the right the forces driving it back to the left, far from being exhausted, have reached their peak; otherwise the reaction could never take place. At one point a person appears to be throwing himself into an external world of projected meanings, but he is being driven to this by a fear of meaninglessness which may break out onto the surface at any moment.

The Being of man is analyzed by Heidegger as the three articulations of "care"—existence, thrownness, and fallenness.[12] We have already said something about the first two. In the terms of our discussion, existence is the basic projecting nature of man. This in turn leads to, or helps explain thrownness. Projecting meaning is casting or throwing oneself ahead into projects understood in terms of human purposes. As we said earlier, projection is by nature blind; that is, we are carried out of ourselves into an external world of objects. We are absorbed in this external "real world" and see ourselves in terms of it.

But just as projection leads to thrownness, so thrownness leads to fallenness. Being blind to projection, throwing ourselves into things, we become lost to ourselves, absorbed in the world. And this is what Heidegger calls man's fallenness. "Dasein is fascinated with its world. Dasein is thus absorbed in the world." [13]

"Falling" is a falling from oneself to the world, a way of disowning oneself. As Magda King describes it, fallenness is " 'falling captive to the world,' ... man's tendency to give himself away to things, to scatter himself in his occupation in company with other people, literally to disown himself." [14] Rather than acknowledge his projecting nature, his responsibility for being-as, man

can turn away from himself, not letting his being fully disclose itself as his own, covering over its finiteness by throwing himself into those 'endless' possibilities that come to him from his world. Existing in this way, man disowns the possibility of the utmost illumination of which his being is capable and falls into the disguise which characterizes his lostness to the world.[15]

If we are led astray in this fashion, it is our own understanding which tempts and seduces us, for the tendency to lose oneself in the world, to assume without thinking the naive realist criterion of meaning, is already contained in the projective nature of understanding.

---

[12] Heidegger, Martin, *Being and Time* (John Macquarrie and Edward Robinson)
[13] *Ibid.*, p. 149.
[14] King, Magda, *Heidegger's Philosophy*, New York: Dell Publishers (Delta Book), 1964, p. 51.
[15] *Ibid.*, p. 57.

Insofar as fallen existence is characterized by a disowning of self, it is "inauthentic." This does not mean that it is immoral, nor that it is unusual or unexpected. Indeed it is the *usual* state of being absorbed in a world of "real things." It is inauthentic in the sense that it is a naive absorption which does not acknowledge its own nature.

One's own *Dasein* ... is encountered proximally and for the most part in terms of the with-world with which we are environmentally concerned. When *Dasein* is absorbed in the world of its concern ... it is not itself.[16]

The tension involved in inauthenticity can be expressed as the tension between private and public meanings. Each man's projection is ultimately personal and private. This does not mean that every individual starts from scratch or that he lives in a private world of his own making. But the very process of learning and acculturation is to assimilate, or make one's own, public forms of projection. This is one of the great difficulties of adolescence, fitting one's own interests, purpose, projects into various socially accepted molds. But insofar as the projection is naive or blind (self-opaque) and insofar as it accomodates itself to public forms, it loses that personal, private character and thus alienates itself from the individual. Alienated from his own projection, the individual begins to see it *as* projection and thus comes face to face with the ultimate meaninglessness of things in themselves.

Thus, projection which makes possible a meaningful world also leads to a sense of meaninglessness. Thought and language are ways of projecting meaning. As such they are basically ways of revealing or disclosing meaning or being-as (Being). But as we lose ourselves in the projection, unaware that we are interpreting the world from a certain standpoint for a certain purpose, understood aspects of the world cease to be revelations of Being and become instead empty clichés. At this point language and thought become a barrier rather than an opening to being-as; we mistake the finger for the moon and lose ourselves in a pre-disclosed, public, average understanding. In the extreme we simply say what is said, think what is thought; but if this does not reveal or disclose the world then it finally becomes meaningless.

One of the most interesting aspects of Heidegger's analysis of

16 Heidegger, *op. cit.*, p. 163.

inauthenticity is his discussion of idle talk. "Idle talk is the possibility of understanding everything without previously making the thing one's own." [17] Here our attention is drawn to the talk rather than the thing talked about; the thing is exhausted, swallowed up and finally replaced by the form of thought.

Consider the expression "the eclipse of God," or "the death of God." At first we may imagine Buber or Nietzsche struggling to give expression to some urgent but vague feeling of man's changing experience of God; then "the eclipse of God," or "the death of God" becomes a powerful conceptual tool, an achievement in disclosing this important phenomenon. But then we settle back, get used to these expressions as they are endlessly discussed on radio, T. V., in news-magazines, schools, etc., until they are reduced to empty shells. In the end, we can no longer recapture Buber's or Nietzsche's achievement. Nor is this limited to the great thinkers. Everyone has experienced the intense excitement of realization—seeing something for the first time. But how stale and disappointing our recorded statement of this same insight will seem a week later as we move on to new problems and fresh solutions!

To have meaning we must project, but projection tends to confuse the interpretation with the thing interpreted. Fastening on to the interpretation as a thing in itself we lose touch both with the world we are trying to interpret and with ourselves as interpreting beings. If Being is being-as, then to lose sight of projection is to cut oneself off from Being. We accept what has previously been revealed, but this ceases to be revelatory; the revealing, projecting, being-as quality is lost and things acquire an uncanny, meaningless guise.

Dialectically, there comes a point at which projection is so successful that it fails, and meaning gives way to meaninglessness. To have meaning we project and this must be naive, unself-conscious, and therefore external, public. But the more public the meaning becomes the more aloof and alien from the center of my own projecting self. At some point I cease to see the world as mine at all. Talk suddenly becomes strange, surrealistic. Just as it ceases to function properly, I see projection for what it is. Even if my thought and language are not original, I must make them my own if they are to reveal some aspect of the world; to understand the world the interpretation must be mine.

17 *Ibid.*, p. 213.

The important point for our analysis is how meaning leads to meaninglessness. Meaning is a human disclosure of some intelligible aspect of the world. This is only possible by projection. But if the projection is a success, it establishes itself publicly; it becomes "what we say." But then it ceases to be a disclosing of some aspect of the world and becomes an accepted feature of reality. But if it is not disclosing Being, it becomes alien, and finally meaningless. Meaning thus leads to meaninglessness; the condition for meaning, projection, becomes the condition for meaninglessness.

The tension within our everyday experience between meaning and meaninglessness which Heidegger analyzes as "fallenness" is *experienced* as dread. We dread authenticity, but we also fear inauthenticity; we are afraid of losing ourselves in an alien world of things and we also shrink from the full implications of accepting our projecting nature. Anxiety is a "fleeing of Dasein in the face of itself." [18] But this very flight presupposes some awareness of authenticity. This subterranean awareness of authenticity is what one flees from and it is also what makes one flee. Similarly, while an alcoholic drinks to *forget* some unacceptable aspect of himself, it is the *awareness* of this aspect which makes him drink. He can neither completely forget nor fully accept himself. So anxiety contains both an incomplete forgetting of self and an incomplete awareness of self. If the self-opaqueness were completely successful or completely unsuccessful, there would be no anxiety but either a mindless acceptance of a given world or a full acceptance of projection and absurdity.

The dialectical relation here is clear. The harder we try to forget, the more we remember. The more we try, the less we succeed. As in a dream, the faster we run away, the less we succeed in escaping. This is because what I run *from* and what *makes* me run is ultimately my own projecting self; trying to forget it simply draws attention to it. What one flees from (is anxious about) and what makes one flee is a recognition that my world is an interpretive achievement, that without my responsibility for projecting meaning, things would fall apart. Anxiety is the fulcrum point holding in balance the opposed forces of meaning and meaninglessness. "As Dasein falls, anxiety brings it back from its absorption in the 'world' "; [19] but as authenticity gains ground, anxiety brings it back to a comfortable absorption in the

[18] *Ibid.*, p. 229.
[19] *Ibid.*, p. 233.

world. As absorption recedes, so does meaning, and we begin to realize that in themselves things are nothing, that their Being (being-as) depends on our projecting possibilities. We begin to see the world *as* world, i.e., as an interpreted world. I no longer see myself in terms of the world, but the world in terms of myself. But this is the meaninglessness which I dread; in bringing us back from inauthentic absorption, anxiety also drives us right back into that absorption. What we dread is that the world is possible only through my projection, that it can fall away and become nothing.

This dialectical tension between meaning and meaninglessness is vividly portrayed in the theater of Beckett and Ionesco. To escape the anxiety of his freedom to project a meaningful world, Ionesco sees man throwing himself into a rational world of his own making,

forced to celebrate his immersion in the absurd with an absurdity, if possible, still greater: the careful and deliberate invention of a pattern of logic to reign where none exists, which he needs and must acquire if he is to preserve his sanity.[20]

But the more successful this imposition of logic on the world, the more alien and absurd it becomes. Having in a sense created existence, language becomes a thing in itself, controlling and victimizing its human makers. Cut off from a responsible, personal disclosure of being-as, language becomes first a veil concealing the world, then an object in its own right and finally, a tyrant. "Speech crumbles, but in another way, words fall like stones, like corpses." [21]

As projection succeeds, it becomes public; but as meaning becomes public, it is no longer a disclosing, no longer one's own—and hence, ironically, alien and meaningless. Meaning is projected—on the one hand this must be a blind, naive projection in which we can lose ourselves, but on the other hand, it must be a disclosing, revealing, which *we do*, something which *we achieve* and are responsible for. These two opposed forces are equally balanced. If either dominates, the result is a sense of meaninglessness—at one extreme a heightened awareness of projection reveals meaninglessness and at the other extreme a thoroughly blind acceptance of an external, public meaning also becomes alien, absurd.

---

[20] Coe, Richard N., *Ionesco*, London: Oliver and Boyd, 1961, p. 38.

[21] Ionesco, Eugene, "The Point of Departure" (L. C. Pronko, trans.), in *Theatre Arts*, vol. 42, June 1958, p. 17.

Their language had become disjointed; the characters disintegrated; their words became meaningless absurdities ... . Words had become empty, noisy shells without meaning ..., (expressing) the automatic quality of language and human behavior, 'empty talk,' speaking because there is nothing personal to say; the absence of any inner life, the mechanical soullessness of daily routine: man totally absorbed in his social context and indistinguishable from it.[22]

The divorce between thought and life. Thought, emptied of life, dries up, shrivels, is no longer thought. For thought is an expression of life, it is identical with life. One can speak without thinking, for this we have clichés.[23]

As language becomes depersonalized it ceases to express emotion. Talking becomes a substitute for feeling, and we become dead to love, tragedy, etc.

The Smiths, the Martins can no longer talk because they can no longer think; they can no longer think *because they can no longer be moved, can no longer feel passions*. They can no longer be; they can 'become' anybody, anything, for, having lost their identity, they assume the identity of others ... they are inter-changeable.[24]

The *awareness* of this situation, however, is a sign of authentic existence. It is an acceptance that the meaningful world is a human projection, ultimately each man's projection. But this is a lonely recognition which alienates the individual from the ordinary man who flees from this awareness, revealing as it does the ultimate absurdity of things.

Destiny has placed man in an impossible situation, and his natural reaction is to shut his eyes and to bury his head in the sand. To the average mortal the merest glimpse of the absurd is disconcerting, if not terrifying.[25]

Indeed, the very act of projecting is already a fleeing from personal responsibility to a public world of accepted standards.

The usual state of existence is one of habit, blindly accepting the public meaning already carved out for us. Only occasionally and for brief periods, are we normally made aware of being-as.

---

[22] Ionesco, Eugene, "The Tragedy of Language," *The Tulane Drama Review*, vol. 4, no. 3, March 1960, p. 12.

[23] Ionesco, Eugene, *Fragments of a Journal* (Jean Stewart, trans.), New York: Grove Press, 1968, p. 30.

[24] Ionesco, "The Tragedy of Language," *op. cit.*, p. 13.

[25] Coe, *op. cit.*, p. 75.

Habit is the ballast that chains the dog to his vomit ... . The world being a projection of the individual's consciousness (an objectification of the individual's will, Schopenhauer would say), the past must be continually renewed, ... The creation of the world did not take place once and for all time, but takes place every day ... . The periods of transition that separate consecutive adaptations represent the perilous zones in the life of the individual ... when for a moment the boredom of living is replaced by the suffering of being.[26]

Man is like an inexperienced tight-rope walker. If he leans too far to one side, accepting his responsibility for being-as, recognizing that Being is being-as, that meaning is projecting, he topples over into meaninglessness. If, to avoid this, he leans to the other side, blindly accepting a fixed public meaning, he alienates himself from the world and this too throws him into meaninglessness. Normally he wobbles uneasily from side to side, giving way to neither extreme entirely, yet constantly, fearfully aware of both. The more he avoids the one, the more he tends to the other. The net result can only be described as the dilemma of "falling."

The mystic's analysis of experience has many affinities with Heidegger. In both the central concept is an attachment to objects of projected meaning in which we lose ourselves. In both there is a recall from this usual fallen, inauthentic state to one of self-awareness, i.e., an awareness of ourselves as projecting a world of meaningful objects. Both emphasize the dialectical tension between meaning and meaninglessness, projection and the awareness of projection, and the impossibility of losing ourselves entirely in a world of projected forms. Where Heidegger speaks of thrownness, the mystic speaks of attachment; where Heidegger speaks of fallenness, the mystic speaks of grasping; and the internal contradictions involved in falling, he describes as the impossibility of ever succeeding in completely grasping, controlling or holding the world. This is beautifully expressed in the Mandingo tale I have used as an epigraph.

No one can hold the world.
You can chase the world until you are tired, until your hands are bleeding.
From the time you are a small child,
from the time you pass through circumcision
until your hair grows white and your mouth
is collapsed and toothless, you may chase the world.

[26] Beckett, Samuel, *Proust*, New York: Grove Press, 1931, p. 8.

But no one will hold Duniya ...
Although you try, you cannot win the world.
The world will win you.[27]

The reason I cannot hold the world is that the world is my projection. To hold the world is to hold myself and this is impossible. To chase after the world of projected meaning is the normal state of human existence; to catch it is impossible.

In *The Way of Zen* Alan Watts expresses this internal contradiction as the cybernetics principle that complete control of events would mean complete lack of control. Where everything is controlled, nothing is controlled. The reason being that complete control would mean control of thought and volition which is ultimately impossible. I may be able to completely control someone else's thoughts and desires but I cannot completely control my own, and this is what complete control of the environment ultimately means—controlling one's own thought and volition.[28]

Of course, we can imagine a small group of determined men controlling through psychological conditioning the thoughts and desires of the rest of the population, and indeed there is widespread concern over this possibility, but to attain complete control would mean controlling the thoughts and desires of the ruling few. But what would this mean? Not that their thought is manipulated by someone else, for this simply pushes the question back one notch—who or what controls *that* person's thought and volition? Nor, for similar reasons, can it be a question of one member controlling the rest. The men must control themselves. But how can they? They might program a computer to psychologically condition themselves to think, feel and behave invariably in certain predetermined ways. But how has this program been set up? In accordance with the thoughts, wishes, desires of the ruling group, and this lies *outside* the system of control. Where the springs of action are controlled, the person is *being controlled*, rather than being *in control*. However, much we regulate and control events, the springs of action must be uncontrolled and spontaneous.

To the extent that we are able to impose meaning and order upon the world we can grasp the world, hold it in our thoughts, manipulate

[27] *Duniya*, a Mandingo tale narrated by Sara Madi Dumbuya, February 1968, Port Loko, Sierra Leone (Mary Howard, trans.).

[28] Watts, Alan W., *The Way of Zen*, New York: A Mentor Book, 1957, pp. 57-58.

it to our ends. Ultimately, as we have said, this projection is based on each man's freedom. But this does not mean we *control* projection. We are responsible for a meaningful world, but we do not sit down and choose what shape the world will take. Ultimately this rests on our form of life—i.e., on our needs and desires as human beings. And this spring of meaning is something given. As Sartre puts it, we are condemned to be free.[29] That we are to have a world at all, that the world will be understood in terms of human projects and intentions is not a matter of choice. We have no option but to project meaning; what we are free to do is to acknowledge or reject that projection and our responsibility for it.

Projection springs from ourselves; thus the more we try to grasp the world the more we try to grasp ourselves. But this is self-frustrating; the hand can hold the ball but it cannot hold itself. The more we try to define meaning the more it slips from our grasp; the more we try to hold the world, the more it eludes us. Like holding a handful of sand, the harder we clutch it the more it slips through our fingers.

In short, whether in everyday experience, scientific investigation, philosophical analysis or religious contemplation, the search for meaning leads to meaninglessness, the conditions necessary for meaning are also necessary for meaninglessness, and meaninglessness is already contained in the traditional "realist" concept of meaning.

[29] Sartre, Jean-Paul, *Being and Nothingness* (H. E. Barnes, trans.), New York: Philosophical Library, 1956, p. 439.

CHAPTER 4

THE TRAGIC SENSE OF MEANINGLESSNESS

In this chapter we examine the tragic response to meaninglessness. Without wishing to resurrect the full-blown fact/value dichotomy, it is often helpful to see opposed points of view as different emotional responses to the same basic phenomenon. John thinks Mary is a brilliant conversationalist, Tim, that she simply talks a lot. Although we cannot ultimately separate the fact about Mary's talking from Tim's evaluation of it, we can see that Tim is unfavorably disposed to Mary's talkativeness, and that, *pace* John, he *need* not respond to it in this way.

So in the case of meaninglessness, it is no secret that meaninglessness is always described in modern European literature in extremely tragic, negative terms. Meaninglessness has been described as mad insane, absurd, ridiculous, senseless, stupid, pointless, mechanical, unreasonable, disconnected, futile, empty and illusory. Similarly, the experience of meaninglessness is described as being uprooted, impotent, abandoned, insignificant, lost and alien.

In Sartre the awareness of meaninglessness is met with a feeling of nausea and revulsion. The human being is *unwanted*, alone among a host of alien or hostile "things" which threaten to choke and crowd him out. For Pascal meaninglessness is seen in terms of a terrifying contingency. For Heidegger it is experienced as dread.

But why *should* the lack of meaning be terrifying, disgusting or unbearably sad? —why should meaninglessness be tragic? The expression "zabool" is totally lacking in meaning, but this does not lead us to throw up our hands in despair or to contemplate suicide. Why does such an extreme response seem appropriate or unavoidable in the case of existential meaninglessness? Certainly, this does not follow simply from the account of meaninglessness as projection. The world is meaningful only in so far as we interpret the world and project meaning; meaning is a feature not of things in themselves, but of being-as. Yes. But what is tragic about that? One need only contrast the 20th-century European response to nothingness with the joyous response of traditional Buddhism to see the gratuitousness —the absurdity—of the modern existentialist response.

Not that this tragic response is altogether irrelevant, but that it does not follow simply from the projective nature of meaning. Something more is required to make such an attitude comprehensible. There must be something else involved in the feeling of nausea, dread, anguish than the mere fact that meaning is projection, that being is being-as. And if we examine our negative attitude toward meaninglessness closely, we will see that this missing ingredient is to be found not so much in what meaninglessness *is* as in what it is *not*. Just as in the previous chapter we saw that arguments for meaninglessness presupposed, and made no sense without, the naive realist criterion of meaning, so here the tragic modern sense of meaninglessness presupposes and makes no sense without the assumption that a meaningful world *ought* to be one in which meaning is simply a part of or identical with reality, i.e., the objectivist criterion of meaning. The modern experience of meaninglessness is a privative response to the *loss, divorce, eclipse* of meaning in the traditional realist sense.

In *Existentialism and Humanism* Sartre contrasts the purpose of the penknife as conceived in the mind of the artisan with the *lack* or *loss* of human purpose in the same or analogous sense. Meaninglessness is thus the perception of the *absence* of anything corresponding to man comparable to the purposeful action of the artisan which could give life meaning. In Wild's discussion meaninglessness is described as "that clashing dissonance between being and meaning that has been widely experienced in our time." [1] Expressed abstractly, the modern experience of meaninglessness is the perception of the clash—i.e., the unfavorable, privative comparison—between meaning as naively identified with reality and meaning as projected, the confrontation of reality as thing-hood and reality as being-as—or rather the *loss* of the one as replaced by the other. The awareness of projection or being-as is tragic because it fails to match up to our *a priori* concept of reality, our concept of the real nature of the thing-in-itself independent of aspects, versions, or ways of looking at things—in short,

[1] Wild, John, "Being, Meaning and the World," in: *Review of Metaphysics*, vol. 18, 1964, p. 427.

substantial reality independent of any subjective interference. Of course, as we suggested in the previous chapter, the concept of the thing itself, which just is what it is, is itself a form of projection, a useful interpretation or handling of certain similarities and differences encountered in everyday experience—necessary to that experience perhaps, as Kant insists, but an interpretation nonetheless.

Projection and being-as bear tragic consequences, then, not of themselves, but by being unfavorably contrasted with a lost sense of meaning inherent in the thing itself, which the awareness that meaning is projection has displaced.

The modern literature of absurdity approaches the clash of meaning and reality in two ways—as the loss of a transcendent source and guarantee of meaning and as the confrontation with a brute matter or thinghood stripped of meaning; man cut off from God and man cut off from Nature.

In Camus the tragic sense of the absurd springs from a comparison of projection with the absolutist ideal of a world of objective, humanly understood meanings. Without this absolutist ideal the fact that we project meaning would *not* lead to the problem of suicide we find in Camus.

The mind's deepest desire ... is an insistance upon familiarity, an appetite for clarity. Understanding the world for a man is reducing it to the human, stamping it with his seal ... . The mind that arises to understand reality can consider itself satisfied only by reducing it to terms of thought.[2]

But this projection must be blind. To satisfy this deepest desire the humanly oriented familiarity and clarity must seem an objective, inseparable feature of reality and not something stamped on it by its human admirers. When thought becomes critically reflective, turning in upon itself, an uneasiness sets in which disturbs the static equilibrium, shattering our security with a familiar world.

So long as the mind keeps silent in the motionless world of its hopes, everything is reflected and arranged in the unity of its nostalagia. But with its first move this world cracks and tumbles: an infinite number of shimmering fragments is offered to the understanding.[3]

The tragic sense of absurdity comes, then, from reading back into this awareness of projection the absolute objectivist ideal of meaning.

[2] Camus, Albert, *The Myth of Sisyphus* (Justin O'Brien, trans.), New York: Vintage Books, 1960, p. 13.
[3] *Ibid.*, p. 14.

Without this we would not see the world as meaningless; indeed, to the extent that it is successful, projection is what makes a meaningful world possible. And this follows ironically from the thesis that meaning is projection. If meaning is projection, then there is as much meaning as there is projection. Since we do project, we do have a meaningful world. If meaning *is* projection, how can projection take away from meaning? Only if projection is understood as displacing the nonprojective ideal of meaning; only where "meaning is projection" is understood to mean "meaning is *not* a real part of the thing itself, but a subjective illusion." Camus is himself keenly aware of this.

I said before that the world is absurd, but I was too hasty. This world in itself is not reasonable, that is all that can be said. But what is absurd is the confrontation of this irrational and the wild longing for clarity whose call echoes in the human heart .... Absurdity consists in the *disproportion* between intention and reality .... The magnitude of the absurdity will be in direct ratio to the distance between the two terms of my comparison .... Absurdity springs from a comparison .... The absurd is essentially a divorce. It lies in neither of the elements compared; it is born of their confrontation .... The world is neither so rational [as the rationalists claim] nor so irrational [as the existentialists claim.] It is unreasonable and only that.[4]

Hence, the tragic, defiant, heroic posture of Camus' heroes, unbending, true to an impossible ideal. But—a suggestion we will take up in the next chapter—is this not an equally absurd position? Is it not itself a form of projection? We cannot say that the world is ugly because there are no objective aesthetic values. Nor can we condemn the world as wicked on the grounds that goodness is a human convention. Likewise, it does not follow that the world is insane just because it lacks human reason.

This is why it is doubtful whether it makes sense to say that projection is illusory. What is projection hiding? To see a chair in the understanding way we normally see it is to interpret it *as* a thing of a certain kind (household furniture for sitting, etc.), and in this sense it is a projected meaning. But this *reveals* rather than conceals the chair. If we press the metaphor of projection and ask what this meaning is projected *onto*, we are brought dangerously close to the outer limits of linguistic meaning. We can, if we wish, venture beyond the ordinary bounds of good sense and suggest that meaning is

[4] *Ibid.*, pp. 16-36.

projected onto the unknowable thing itself, but we can*not* say it is projected onto the *chair* for the chair only arises *with* the act of projection.

Ionesco's account of meaninglessness is as uncompromisingly grim as Camus's

I have no other image of the world except those of evanescence and brutality, vanity and rage, nothingness, useless hatred ... vain and sordid fury, cries suddenly stifled by silence, shadows engulfed forever in the night.[5]

But as he suggests in his remarks on *The Chairs*, this description is an implicit comparison with a lost ideal, understandable only by its *absence*. The subject of the play is

the chairs themselves; that is to say, the *absence* of people, the *absence* of the emperor, the *absence* of God, the *absence* of Matter, the *un*reality of the world, metaphysical emptiness. The theme of the play is nothingness.[6]

But a nothingness which can only be felt as the absence of something expected or desired.

Like Camus and Sartre, Ionesco's denunciation of the absurdity of life seems to presuppose the possibility of rising above it in some way.

If I denounce the absurd, I transcend the absurd by the very fact of my denunciation. For by what right should I declare a thing to be absurd, unless I had before me the image—whether sharply or vaguely defined, no matter—of something that was *not* absurd?[7]

The denunciation of absurdity is only possible, in other words, by means of an implied contrast with the unattainable goal of objective meaning. But if we are irretrievably stuck in the midst of absurdity, as all these writers maintain, how do we transcend it? How is it possible to defy death in the manner of Camus's heroes or to aspire, in Heideggerian terms, to an "authentic" life? If this is possible at all it is only from what I described earlier as the absolutist point of view. When we are engaged in things in a mundane context, we are not aware of, and so cannot condemn, meaninglessness. But when, on rare occasions, we stand back and look down on things from an

    [5] Ionesco, Eugene, "Lorsque j'écris ...," in: Esslin, Martin, *The Theatre of the Absurd*. Harmondsworth, England: Penguin Books, 1968, p. 132.

    [6] Ionesco, Eugene, "Letter to Sylvain Dhomme," *Ibid.*, p. 149.

    [7] Ionesco, Eugene in conversation with George Lerminier, "Dialogue avec Ionesco," in: Coe, Richard N., *Ionesco*, London: Oliver and Boyd, Ltd., 1961, p. 73.

Olympian height, those same things appear pointless and absurd. It is from this perspective that existentialist writers describe man's absurd existence. But in what sense is this authentic? Is this absolutist perspective any less a projection, is this contrast any less an interpretation than that of the average man? Is the absolutist perspective from which the absurdity of the world is condemned any truer or more basic or more genuine than the mundane attitude of everyday existence? Is "the lucid perception of meaninglessness ... itself a meaningful—the only meaningful—act," as Coe suggests? [8] Or, is this, as Ionesco seems to affirm at times, itself an absurd act?

We cannot soar above it all, we cannot be superior to the Divinity ... . That's piece of folly ... . We cannot reject the world ... . To say that the world is absurd is equally ridiculous ... . It is absurd to say that the world is absurd. [9]

If *all* thought is projection, then how do we (in what sense do we) exclude the absolutist denunciation? But, if this too is projective, then what sense can we make of authentic existence, fully aware of its absurdity, rejecting, rising above it? This paradox, which is not unlike the Buddhist paradox of wanting not to want anything, or of trying to become a Buddha when one already is one, is central to existentialist thought. In short, the question is, can one stand outside the general absurdity of things and cast judgment on it? And if not, what is the point of trying to "authentically" understand oneself and one's relation to a world of meaningful objects? In Chapter 5 we will develop as a kind of solution to the problem of meaninglessness the theme that the awareness of projection and absurdity is itself an absurd projection—that to literally rise up against the world is an illusion. The awareness of projection is a form of projection; the disgust with meaninglessness is itself meaningless. All perceptions are relatively meaningless in the naive realist sense of meaning and all are relatively meaningful in the projection sense of meaning.

Like Ionesco, Adamov also views meaninglessness from the perspective of an absolute, transcendent meaning no longer accessible to us. The world *must* have some transcendent meaning which guarantees a final purpose to the world as a whole. The structure of the world itself is not sufficient on this view to guarantee meaning, and

---

[8] Coe, *Ibid.*, p. 65.

[9] Ionesco, Eugene, *Fragments of a Journal* (Jean Stewart, trans.), New York: Grove Press, 1968, p. 83.

indeed in the absence of any transcendent source of meaning the structure of the world collapses and things fall apart. As Adamov wrote in "Pain," "at the heart of myself there is mutilation, separation," and this separation can only be understood as standing over against the palpable image of wholeness always just beyond our grasp, like the horizon which we see but can never reach.[10]

It is this negative, privative awareness which makes meaninglessness possible. As Sartre puts it, man is a "hole in Being ... through which nothingness enters the world." [11] Like a cup without a handle, man is incomplete, lacking something, and it is through this *gap* or *break* in man's existence that the thought of what he is *not* (hence nothingness) can enter.

The lack of an assigned meaning to man's existence, or to the life of a particular man, is tragic only by contrast with a complete, transcendent meaning. Meaninglessness must be seen as a *failed* meaning, as the demise or eclipse of meaning. This is what invites the tragic response. Adamov says,

Behind its visible appearances, life hides a meaning that is eternally inaccessible to penetration by the spirit, that seeks for its discovery, caught in the dilemma of being aware that it is impossible to renounce the hopeless quest.[12]

What is tragic in this account, as Esslin points out, is

the awareness that there may be a meaning but that it will never be found ... . Any conviction that the world is wholly absurd would lack this tragic element.[13]

As Camus said, "this world in itself is not reasonable, that is all that can be said;" [14] meaning is projection, being is being-as, we have no right to say any more than this.

Similarly, in Beckett, it is the pointless *waiting*, the useless but not quite extinguished *hoping* which is so agonizing; it is the idea that Godot will come which casts a shadow on the alogical fact of man's existence. The solution, as Beckett of all these writers comes closest to realizing, is not for Godot to come but for us to give up the idea that he might or ought to come—though this is far more difficult.

---

[10] Adamov, Arthur, "The Endless Humiliation" (Richard Howard, trans.), New York: *Evergreen Review*, vol. 2, no. 8, 1959, p. 66.

[11] Sartre, Jean-Paul, *Being and Nothingness* (H. E. Barnes, trans.), New York: Philosophical Library, 1956, p. 24.

[12] Adamov, Arthur, "Une fin et un commencement," in: Esslin, *op. cit.*, p. 93.

[13] Esslin, *Ibid.*

[14] Camus, *op. cit.*

For to know is nothing, not to want to know anything likewise, but to be beyond knowing anything, that is when peace enters in, to the soul of the incurious seeker.[15]

I suggested earlier that there are two ways of portraying the clash between meaning and reality in the modern literature of absurdity. If we characterize the first, which we have been discussing up to now, as man without God, we may describe the second as man without Nature. This is the idea, much discussed, of alienation and estrangement. Stripped of meaning, the objects of the external world become strange, even hostile, and man is alienated from the very world in which he lives, thus acquiring the guise of an uncrowned king, a lost god (as Plato also described man),

surrounded, captivated, and hemmed in on all sides by being which to him is opaque or hostile, and which threatens him because of its nearness and its irruption,[16]

the encroachment of a meaningless reality on subjectivity. But, again, the horror of this encroachment only makes sense as contrasted with a humanly interpreted world of nonprojected, i.e., objective, yet humanly understood meanings. Being is being-as, meaning is projection; the world as we know it is an interpreted world, a human achievement, and without projection and being-as, the world itself (though this is strictly speaking something of a contradiction in terms) is without meaning. But there is nothing here of horror or dread. The uninterpreted object doesn't mean anything; until we have interpreted it, we don't understand it. To understand something we must understand it—that is all!

It does not follow from this that external reality is "grotesque, headstrong, repugnant, gross and unbearable;" that it should "inconvenience, embarrass, confuse, or alarm us," or make us feel "in the way," as Sartre insists.[17] Indeed to respond in this way can only be understood by contrast with our accustomed response to a world of humanly interpreted meanings. It is not simply that man finds the world actually stripped of meaning. This is at best an exceedingly rare experience even for someone of Antoine's sensibilities and

[15] Beckett, Samuel, *Molloy*, London: Calder and Boyars (A Juniper Book), 1966, p. 68.

[16] Mounier, Emmanuel, *Existentialist Philosophies*, London: Rockliff, 1948, p. 36.

[17] Sartre, Jean-Paul, *Nausea* (Lloyd Alexander, trans.), Norfolk, Connecticut: New Directions Books, 1959, pp. 169-180.

detached circumstances. Even for the existentialist "outsider" the world we normally experience is (almost by definition) a meaningful, humanly interpreted world. The experience of meaninglessness is rather the reflection that this interpreted world is a projected world, that being is being-as, that *in themselves* things are meaningless, not that they normally appear so. Thus the tragic contrast is not between things which appear meaningful and things which suddenly appear totally unrecognizable, but that between the *projected* meaningfulness of things and the naively *nonprojective* ideal of meaning identical with the things themselves. It is the implied contrast with meaning as the essential nature of the thing itself which paralyzes the heart with fear.

The tragic contrast between man and an alien world of "things" is ascribed by Heidegger and Jaspers to man's "transcendence." The being of man, "existence," is understood by way of contrast with the being of something like a stone. A stone just is, it doesn't know that it exists, nor does it foresee what it might become. It cannot understand itself in terms of an idea, hope or desire realizable by planning and thoughtful action. In this sense it is stuck in what it is; it cannot rise above this. In the technical language of existentialism, its essence preceeds its existence. But man is different; he understands and judges his existence and that of other things. He can experience dissatisfaction with the *status quo* and imagine preferable alternatives some of which he can bring into being through his own efforts. As Heidegger puts it, man understands himself primarily in his throwness, in terms of projects which he conceives purposively. Even where he can't bring about change, he knows how things stand and he can imagine what they might be like. In this sense, man transcends his existence, he rises above mere being.

But this is not a triumphal transcendence. Man still finds himself plunked down in an alien world on which he is dependent and into which he is drawn out of himself. He has not chosen to be nor to be in this particular world of objects which do not know and judge their own being and which are recalcitrant to his ends and projects. Ultimately he knows he is part of this world and that he will finally be dragged down by and into the world through fallenness and death. He transcends the world of mere things in understanding, in evaluation, but he does not rise above the world like a god standing apart from the world. Again, he is stuck in between complete godlike transcendence and utter stonelike immanence. And this is what is tragic. If he were a stone, or even the cow in Nietzsche's *Use and Abuse of History*, he would not be unhappy or dissatisfied. If he were a god, surveying all, judging all, complete master of his own destiny, he would not be unhappy. But he is neither; he is struck in the world and he is dissatisfied.

In this sense man's being is flawed, cracked, incomplete; it is not a whole or complete thing as are in different ways stones and gods. The stone is complete in itself, finished and thus static; the being of man is constantly reaching out beyond itself and is thus dynamic and necessarily incomplete. Thus man's awareness of being, his projection, does not add anything to being, but ironically diminishes it, calling it into question, upsetting its static balance, taking away from its fullness. Again, the tragic consequence consists in the unhappy tension between the being of the stone which man can neither accept nor completely rise above and the being of the gods to which he aspires but can never achieve. Man's transcendence is limited to perceiving this tension and being dissatisfied with it.

The human being is not what the eternal and immutable laws of matter has decreed that he should be; he is what he has decided to be ... . Nevertheless, there is inertia in being ... . Sartre's paradox ... consists in creating out of this movement of being, not the effect of accomplishment, but the effect of impotence ... . *Being-in-itself* ... consists of a sort of fulness. Yet, it is a dead sort of fulness ... . Being-in-oneself is what it is in a stupid way, with no recoil upon itself and without any over-extension in advance of itself. It is self-centered, meaningless to itself, huge, ingenuous, too solid, and, in the opinion of the world, unwanted and superfluous ... whence arises Nausea, that vague and stifling uneasiness ... . The human being, the conscious being, the *being-for-oneself*, is not a super-being, but a 'decompression of being.' He does not fully coincide with himself ... . But this decompression is not possible until a crack has developed in being, a crack into which nothingness worms its way. The establishment of being thus constitutes a 'gap in being;' it creates a doubt about being; it constitutes a victory for nothingness.[18]

Much ink has been shed on the existentialist theory of negation, though there is still a great deal of misunderstanding surrounding it. Yet if we can make sense of this view of negation, we will have succeeded in clarifying the tragic response to meaninglessness, for the sense of nothingness is possible only by man's ability to perceive negation. Negation, Sartre and Heidegger want to say, is not an objective feature of the world. In this respect they are in full agree-

[18] Mounier, *op. cit.*, pp. 29-31.

ment with Parmenides. Negation is rather a human perception of something missing, something absent—something which ought to be there or which we expect to be there but is not. It is this idea which lies behind the oracular sayings that negation is nothing, that negation does nothing, that it negates nothing, and so on. It is not a thing in itself, a force in its own right, but a human way of seeing rooted in man's projective, thrown nature. Man understands the world in terms of projects, possibilities; he can foresee what might exist but does not now exist. He sees what does exist in terms of what it needs, lacks, or requires. He looks at the table and says, "We need dessert spoons." He looks in at the cafe and says, "Bill's not here." This is essentially a transcendental analysis. We are asking what makes negation possible, what conditions must be present before words like "not" or "nothing" can make any sense, and the answer lies in man's ability to perceive things in terms of what they might become, to look ahead and to throw himself ahead of himself. The point is, there is no real absence or gap in being; in themselves there is no negation or nothingness; there is only a falling away from human concepts and desires. There is a table with things on it, there is a café with people, tables, chairs, etc., in it. There is no "nothing" here. The question of "nothing" doesn't arise until someone—some person—asks, "Where are the spoons?" "Where is Bill?" Only then do we get a "not."

Similarly when you say someone no longer exists, that he is no more, you mean he has died, and this only makes sense given the concept of a living person. Things are constantly changing in various ways; some of these changes do not affect a thing's existence while other changes do. Bill survives the loss of his hair, but not the loss of his heartbeat. A piece of wood is sawed in half and the wood is still there; it is ground into pulp and made into paper and the wood has ceased to exist. Ironically, what determines at what point a thing has ceased to exist is our *concept* of that thing. Things only exist or cease to exist *as* this or that. Only projected being-as can exist, cease to exist or be a particular thing. Without being-as, without human concepts, no thing would either exist or cease to exist. This is not an endorsement for idealism. It does not mean that in the absence of human beings there would be nothing in the world at all. What it means is that it is only by virtue of concepts that we can say that *this* or *that* exists or ceases to exist; only with human concepts and projection do we get the comprehensible distinction between existence and non-existence. Without human concepts we could point to the world and say that there is "all that," but we could not say *what* there is; we could not say there is this rather than that; we could not say that such and such used to exist but had now ceased to exist.

Thus, a necessary condition for the recognition that something is not present, that this or that doesn't exist is the privative contrast with some human ideal or concept. This is the source of the uniquely human possibility of being dissatisfied with the *status quo* and the foundation for the tragic sense of nothingness. We are contrasting how we conceive things might be with how we understand they actually are. But since the concept with which we contrast projection is itself projection, the tragic sense of meaninglessness depends entirely on an ideal we have ourselves erected. It depends on the reification of projected concepts, the clash between a blindly projected ideal of being as substantial reality or thinghood and the awareness that being is being-as. In the experience of meaninglessness we contrast projected meaning with the thing in itself which is itself the ultimate projection and the foundation for the rest.

CHAPTER 5

BACK TO SQUARE ONE

Must the awareness of projection be tragic? Only, as we saw in the last chapter, if it is unfavorably contrasted with the nonprojective ideal of objective meaning. The tragedy, as Esslin points out, is "the awareness that there may be a meaning but that it will never be found." [1] As Ionesco says, "by what right should I declare a thing absurd unless I had before me the image ... of something that was *not* absurd?" [2] Without this realist ideal the world would be seen as an interpreted world, but it would not be felt as absurd, senseless or stupid. Without the nonprojective identification of meaning with reality the awareness that meaning is projection would be an awareness of the *nature* of meaning—not its *loss*. As Esslin puts it, "Any conviction that the world is wholly absurd would lack this tragic element." [3]

The question, therefore, is whether it is possible to renounce the objectivist ideal of nonprojected meaning and embrace completely the projective nature of man and the interpreted character of the world? Can we "negate ... this desire for unity, this longing to solve, this need for clarity and cohesion," which Camus rhetorically suggests we cannot? [4] Is it "impossible," as Adamov believes, "to renounce the hopeless quest?" [5] Can we, by renouncing the nonprojective

[1] Esslin, Martin, *The Theatre of the Absurd*, Harmondsworth, England: Penguin Books, Ltd., 1968, p. 93.

[2] Ionesco, Eugene, in conversation with George Lerminier, "Dialogue avec Ionesco," in: Coe, Richard N., *Ionesco*, London: Oliver and Boyd, Ltd., 1961, p. 73.

[3] Esslin, *op. cit.*

[4] Camus, Albert, *The Myth of Sisyphus* (Justin O'Brien, trans.), New York: Vintage Books, 1960, p. 38.

[5] Adamov, Arthur, "The Endless Humiliation" (Richard Howard, trans.), *Evergreen Review*, vol. 2, no. 8, 1959, p. 66.

ideal of meaning, find a positive, constructive side to the sheer meaninglessness of things in themselves? In this final chapter I want to explore this possibility.

We have already dropped certain hints and pointers along the way which we must now gather together and place before us in a definitive and affirmative manner. The first thing to be said in renouncing non-projective meaning is that this is a false and impossible ideal. There is no alternative to projection, nothing else we can *do* but project meaning and nothing we can even *conceive* to contrast with projection. Hence the awareness that meaning is projection, that being is being-as, is not the tragic denial that the world falls short of some real but unattainable goal; it is simply the realization of the conditions necessary for a meaningful world of human experience.

In itself there is nothing abhorent about projection, indeed its value lies precisely in the fact that it makes possible a meaningful world. What is bad is the false ideal of nonprojective meaning. But this ideal is not only impossible; it is itself a form of projection, a simplified reduction of ordinary experience into fixed categories of things and their natures. The awareness of projection is the realization that this is only a convenient way of speaking which does not strictly or literally correspond with reality. It is the realization that the "nature" of an object is an interpretation revealed by projection, that the thing in itself has no meaning apart from some interpretation.

The second thing to be noted is that the point of view from which this realization is made, the absolutist point of view from which Existentialist writers view the tragic sense of meaninglessness, is no better or truer than the mundane point of view which reveals the interrelated meaning of things in everyday life. From the absolutist point of view, *sub specie aeternatatis*, things are meaningless; from the mundane point of view, they are meaningful. Both points of view are valid; both statements true from the appropriate standpoint. The irony is that things *are* meaningful to me just because I am engaged in them here and now, and it is also true that in the broader perspective they are *not* meaningful. By concentrating on the latter point of view, "what will it matter 5000 years from now," the Existentialists have made it seem as though absurdity is the last word. But this is only half the story. If we stand back from the normal course of events, we relinquish that sense of connectedness with things, and objects lose what meaning they previously had for us.

When we re-enter the ordinary milieu, things again become meaningful.

This is why it is wrong to suppose, as some Existentialists have
done, that the awareness of absurdity or the revolt against it transcends
absurdity. The heroic posture of Camus' heroes defying the absurdity
of ordinary existence is not the one meaningful act with which we
contrast the senseless routine of everyday life. The awareness of
absurdity is just as absurd as the plain man's naive acceptance of
the meaningfulness of things—and just as meaningful. As an intelligible aspect of the world exhibited from a particular human point
of view, both the acceptance and the rejection of absurdity are
equally meaningful; as interpretations of the world both are equally
projections, and in *this* sense, meaningless. The revolt against absurdity, as Coe points out, is "again absurdity, raised to the n-th degree." [6]
To see that all is ultimately meaningless is a true reflection from the
absolutist point of view, but it does not reveal the thing as it really is,
shorn of all human interpretations, for it is itself a human achievement,
an interpretation with a distinct cultural (late Romantic) background.
We rise above the meaninglessness of life by becoming aware of it,
not by escaping it. As Coe says of Ionesco, "between the total and
the sham reality there is, in the final analysis, no effective contrast.
Both are gratituitous, both are void, both are meaningless." [7] Because
Ionesco never renounced the ideal of nonprojective meaning and
the priority of the absolutist perspective, he could not see that both
are equally meaningful as well.

The world as we know it is a recognizable world of meaningful
items bound together into a more or less familiar system. In themselves things have no meaning, but the world we know and experience
is a world which we interpret and understand in terms of human
concepts and forms of thought. The world in itself is not something
we *could* experience; the world we can experience is by that very
token a world we experience in terms of human concepts and categories. Thus to say that the world in itself is meaningless is really
a tautology—it is saying that the world minus human reason and
interpretation is a world without reason and interpretation. On the
other hand, to say that the world we know and experience is reasonable and meaningful is also tautology—it is saying that the world

---

[6] Coe, *op. cit.*, p. 75.
[7] *Ibid.*, p. 61.

which we interpret and explain to ourselves is an interpreted and explainable world. And since this is the world we are really concerned about, being the one we actually live and move about in, the problem of meaninglessness properly understood does not have the enormous tragic proportions which it is generally reputed to have.

The solution to the contradictions we saw in Nietzsche's or Coleridge's or Korzybski's vacillating accounts of the projective nature of meaning is to admit that meaning is projection and to deduce from this the consequence that *because* we project, there *is* meaning. Projection, in other words, implies meaning (in the sense of projection) as well as meaninglessness (in the non-projection sense). The trick is to know we are projecting and go right on doing so—to enjoy a meaningful world knowing that it is an interpreted world, to embrace being knowing it is being-as, to have a meaningful human world knowing that in themselves things are meaningless.

I said earlier that there were two senses of meaning, having a world and the nonprojective ideal; and equally two senses of meaninglessness, the loss of a world and the awareness of projection. In the past philosophers have argued that the awareness of projection is intolerable because it results in the loss of a world. What I have tried to show, on the contrary, is that meaninglessness in the sense of the loss of a world is due precisely to the nonprojective concept of meaning. Where philosophers have argued that meaning is only possible on a nonprojective identification of meaning and reality, I have tried to show that it is projection which makes meaning possible. Thus, we avoid meaninglessness in the tragic sense of things falling apart precisely because we *accept* meaninglessness in the sense of projection. We accept meaninglessness, in other words, only in the sense that we recognize the meaningfulness of the interpreted world of human experience.

Thus we reject meaninglessness in the only sense in which it hurts, the loss of a coherent world, and we accept meaninglessness only in the sense that there is no meaning without projection. We reject the meaninglessness of things as we experience them, and accept only the meaninglessness of the hypothetical thing-in-itself. Putting it the other way round, we accept the meaningfulness of the world we live in and reject only the contradictory idea of the meaningfulness of things in themselves.

This indicates what I wish to convey finally by the "meaning of meaninglessness"—the meaning *contained in* and *presupposed by* meaninglessness. Meaninglessness in the tragic Existentialist sense is based on the nonprojection idea of meaning and would be impossible without this, as we saw in Chapter 4. But the meaninglessness of things in themselves also implies the meaningfulness of things in the projected world of everyday experience, and this is also the meaning of meaninglessness. Equally, we could speak of the meaninglessness within meaning, that meaning is possible only through projection, that is, only on condition that things in themselves are meaningless. The irony of meaning is that the nonprojective ideal of meaning logically commits one to the tragic sense of meaninglessness, while projective meaning is simply one way of describing the meaninglessness of things in themselves. The tragic sense of meaninglessness is bound up with the nonprojection idea of meaning, while the meaning of the world we actually live in is tied to the meaninglessness of the thing in itself.

Looked at in this way, the awareness of meaninglessness ceases to be a demoralizing, debilitating, tragic reflection and becomes instead simply the awareness of the nature of meaning. "Meaning is projection" has two handles, we may say: that things in themselves are meaningless and that things in the world as we conceive it are meaningful. The Existentialists have grabbed hold of the first, ignoring the second. We must now offset this imbalance by embracing both, as two sides of the same coin. To say that meaning is projection is to say that meaning is a matter of interpretation, a human achievement; and this is just to say that without interpretation, without some limited human perspective, things in themselves are meaningless. And this puts meaninglessness in a more manageable and less tragic perspective.

As we have seen, some philosophers and critics have come close to the position I am developing though none has endorsed it completely. Ionesco sees that there is no human posture or attitude which is not an extension and projection of man's self. But he retains the ideal of objective meaning in terms of which he castigates all life and experience as tragically senseless and absurd. Beckett sees the goal of a complete acceptance of projection which would take away its tragic element of absurdity, yet his own vision is pervaded by the absolutist gaze out and beyond toward an ideal but nonexistent final meaning. Heidegger sees that we are completely and irremovably immersed in fallenness, but he nonetheless postulates an "authentic" mode of existence which seems somehow to transcend the senselessness of life. "Authentic" existence, like transcendence, *is* a possible mode of human existence but only in the sense of our being aware of and owning up to our own projective nature—not in the sense of overcoming our absorption in a world of projected meanings.

Bergson recognized that all analytic, discursive thought was a projection of human attitudes and categories, but he felt this was a distortion of reality with which he contrasted intuitive thought which did not interpret, and hence distort, reality but entered directly into the thing as it is in itself. There *is* a type of thought we may call intuitive, but it differs from scientific, discursive thought, not in the absence of interpretative categories, but in a more subtle and less explicit form of interpretation. Even in intuition one approaches the object from a human point of view and thus sees it in a particular way which is a human achievement. The point of view may be more sympathetic, but it is nonetheless an adopted point of view.

Closest to the position developed here is probably Husserl's phenomenological analysis. Husserl points out how in everyday cognition objects appear as simply given; that is, no notice is paid to *how* they are given in cognition, rather the fact that we cognize them is simply assumed or taken for granted. This is what Heidegger calls our lostness and fallenness in the world. When traditional philosophy gets round to examining this ordinary cognition, it is baffled how such a thing is even possible. And this is precisely because cognition has never been brought to conscious self-reflection. The philosopher argues that true cognition must somehow take hold of the object as it is in itself. But then, as it becomes clear that this is scarcely possible except through the intermediary of thought, it seems as though a barrier to true cognition has been erected within cognition itself. But this presupposes an idea of true cognition which simply takes cognition for granted. The ideal of cognition, in other words, simply takes it for granted that objects are just given in cognition, simply handed over *in toto*, without clarifying how this takes place. Since it is difficult, upon reflection, to see how this *can* take place, scepticism is the natural offshoot of this traditional approach.

Without criticising cognition in terms of any pre-conceived ideal, Husserl seeks to observe cognition in the very act, so to speak, to cognize as one *normally* does but to become *aware* of our doing so. What this reveals, in Husserl's famous reductive analysis, is that objects only appear in cognition as part of an intentional relation of thought toward its object. Cognition and the object of thought arise together through our directing attention to various aspects of things from certain human points of view, which Heidegger goes on to develop in terms of purposive human projects. What Husserl is led to see, in other words, is that cognition is only possible through projection. But this is not a criticism of cognition, it is simply an analysis of it. As an analysis of cognition it cannot, therefore, deny or cast doubt upon cognition. In ordinary experience we project without knowing we do so; hence things are meaningful and appear as simply given. In phenomenological reflection, we become *aware* that meaning is projection and that things *seem* to be given because we are *not* normally aware of this projection. But this is no more a denial of meaning than recognition that one is singing and an awareness of the conditions necessary for singing imply that one is *not* singing. What we give up on the phenomenological analysis is the naive assumption that meanings are just given—not meaning itself. The point is that awareness of the nature of something, be it meaning, cognition, or whatever, does not and indeed cannot negate that thing. It is simply a shift from a naive, unreflective acceptance of X to a reflective awareness of X.

And so, in a sense, there is a return to square one. At first we naively suppose that things are meaningful because meaning non-projectively attaches itself to objects. Later when we discover that this is not the case, that meaning is projection, we tend to scepticism, idealism and meaninglessness. But this is logically inconsistent; when we complete the argument at last, we reaffirm that things are meaningful precisely *because* we project meaning. So, we're back where we started, but with this important difference in our attitude toward projection. In the first case we project blindly; in the second case, reluctantly, despairingly; in the third case, we accept projection knowingly and with responsibility. Thus, there is no alternative to projection: only differing interpretations of it—the wrong interpretation that it is the source of meaninglessness and the correct interpretation that it is the source of meaning.

Neither is there any alternative to projection in Heidegger's account. In *Being and Time* there is nothing with which to contrast being-as, or rather being-as (Being) is contrasted precisely with "nothing." "Nothing" in Heidegger is set off against both real and ideal Being. Nothing is not the absence of substantial matter but the absence of meaning. If something has character (meaning) and can be described (has being-as), if, that is, it answers to the question "what is it?' then it is something and has Being in Heidegger's sense, whether real or imaginary. This brings out the curious irony in words like "being." In the sense of being-as Being is something; in the sense of the real thing in itself Being is nothing. This or something like it is what the Buddhists mean when they characterize reality as emptiness or nothingness, i.e., lacking in intrinsic human meanings. Insofar as these meanings by definition have content, they are "something;" insofar as they are reified, hypostatized, they are nothing (i.e., nothing in themselves, nothing in a world independent of human projection).

There is a reverse irony in the case of "reality." In the sense of its recognizable shape or character, the real thing in itself is nothing —again, this or something like it is what the Buddhists mean by Suchness, the characterless nature of what is, the fact that reality is never caught in the net of our thought. But as a reference point beyond thought to which our interpretations refer, it is something. Reality is something we-can't-say-what, it's that-which we seek to understand and strive to know better and better in a never-ending assault, but which, necessarily, we cannot understand outside of some interpretation.

Earlier on, in discussing Heidegger, we said that all thought and language is standpoint- or culture-bound. This means that the real thing itself cannot be known as such. In discussing Wild, however, we found a place in our language for "reality" which Heidegger seems to overlook. As a relative and regulative concept, we speak of interpretations of reality and of trying to learn what "really happened." We know there is a real world out there, but we cannot say what it is like except in terms of human categories of thought. On the one hand we realize that reality can only be apprehended as interpreted being-as; but on the other hand we are equally aware that no thought can ever exhaust the object. The first leads to the idea that Being is being-as, that meaning and Being are correlative concepts; the second, to the idea that reality is nonetheless distinct from Being (meaning). The net result is a sense of reality as Suchness, a reality we know exists and to which we can point but which we know we can never characterize except partially by exhibiting various recognizable facets of it from certain human points of view.

On the one hand to recognize the limitations of thought is to see that we are standpoint- and culture-bound, that we cannot *grasp* a world beyond human concepts and interpretations, that the world we do understand is an interpreted world. On the other hand recognition of the limitations of thought is the realization that no thought is identical or interchangeable with its object, that reality, therefore transcends being-as. Logically the concept of reality is regulative *within* the standpoint-bound world of being-as. That which we understand only vaguely and wish to understand better we refer to relatively as the reality to be clarified. It is itself cognized reality, i.e., being-as, but relative to the desired clarification it is the object to which thought is directed. Existentially, reality is experienced as the horizon which we can never grasp but which nonetheless determines our attitudes and behavior in trying to discover the truth.

Existentially, a person is aware of himself as possessing limited information or insight about a certain object. He knows he doesn't understand the object thoroughly and he is aware of a desire to probe deeper, to explore further, to find out more about the object. Of course, by hypothesis he doesn't understand what it is about this object that he doesn't know. To this extent he is aware that he is locked up within his own skin, so to speak. At the same time he is aware that this information does not exhaust the object and to *that* extent the idea of the thing itself—over and above his own limited vision of it—enters his consciousness. Not as an idea he could define or in any way describe, but only as an "it," a "that" to which he points. What is it we want to understand when we try to interpret the world? "That, all that," is all we can say, pointing to a world beyond.

This regulative idea of reality we have called, following the Buddhists, Suchness. In the sense in which being-as is something (meaning), Suchness is nothing. "*What* is it?' "Nothing," i.e., no thought' is fully adequate to it. In the sense in which Suchness is real (it is there, the object of our thought), being-as is nothing. The nonprojective idea of meaning, whether naively presupposed in common sense or affirmed philosophically, misses both these points. By identifying meaning with reality (assuming the thing just *is* what we *call* it) the objectivist criterion of meaning falsely reifies its own thoughts, mistakes the finger which points for the moon to which it points, fails, in other words, to see that thoughts are not their objects. But by identifying meaning with reality, the objectivist criterion of meaning also assumes that reality is fixed, exhausted by its essential meaning. The mistake is two-fold, first to suppose that meanings are objectively real things in themselves, and second, and correlatively, to suppose that the thing itself is identical with its meaning (or nature). Crudely put, the first objectifies thought, the second subjectifies reality.

The idea of reality as Suchness is a corrective to the idealist tendencies implied in the idea that Being is being-as. Against Korzybski and others who held that thought necessarily distorts reality, Urban argues that thought cannot distort reality since it is "custom-made" to fit its own interpreted culture-bound object.[8] Korzybski emphasizes the distinctness of meaning and reality; Urban, their conformity. But both are right (and both wrong) in different ways. Urban is right in the sense that meaning necessarily conforms to being-as; Korzybski is equally right in the sense that meaning does *not* conform to reality, or Suchness. Urban is right in denying that we can meaningfully speak of thought distorting reality, but he is wrong in his assumption that "reality" has no place in our thought and language. Korzybski is wrong in assuming that because thought is correlative with being-as it distorts and falsifies reality, but he is right in seeing that our concept of truth implies degrees of conformity with reality, the rejection of false views of the world, and especially the never-ending quest to get a better view of the world.

Urban's analysis suggests an idealist interpretation which trivializes the problem of truth. If thought is culture-bound and necessarily conforms to its culture-bound object, then truth is equally culture-bound and relative to whatever interpretation one can put on reality. But this ignores the fact that we can become dissatisfied with our own interpretation of events which we may find in conflict with the facts. We live in an interpreted world, yes; but we also have a sense of an only partially disclosed reality to which our interpretation has some responsibility. Obviously one can't think what lies beyond thought, but one can be and is aware of the need to probe deeper, to get a fuller or more accurate or less biased view of the affair. One never arrives at the end of this search, but this sort of quest clearly plays an important part in our approach to truth. The human situation in regard to truth is to be standpoint-bound and also *know* that one is standpoint-bound, to be limited in one's thought and also to know these limitations. But as Kant saw, to realize the limitations of thought is to see both that thought is conceptually limited *and*

8 Urban, W. M., *Language and Reality*, London: George Allen and Unwin, 1939.

that reality is not. To be aware of a limit is to have some awareness of what lies beyond that limit.

Of course, this involves the paradox that we are aware of something which is strictly inconceivable. But this is not merely a *conceptual* dilemma; it is primarily an existential paradox of the human situation, to know that one doesn't know all there is to know about a certain thing, to strive to increase one's knowledge aware that one will never get beyond a partial, more or less adequate human interpretation of it. An historian approaches the study of some event, whether the 1917 Russian Revolution or the assassination of John Kennedy, with an understanding of certain more or less objective facts which do not however in themselves comprise an intelligible story or account of the event. He is also familiar with the various competing interpretations, and he probably has a certain predisposition for one over the others. But if he is a good historian he does not rest content with his favorite interpretation. He is nagged by the feeling that all are more or less adequate and all more or less inadequate and he is pressed on by this nagging awareness to get to the bottom of the matter, to find out what really happened. He interviews more witnesses; he reviews all the data again and again and gradually begins to refine, fill in, reject certain parts and include other parts of one or other of these interpretations or to begin to work out a new interpretation which takes account of the elements of truth in each of the others. He does, then, have a sense of responsibility to a reality which he does not fully understand but which is the object of his search. He also has a sense of zeroing in on this reality, getting closer and closer to it. He feels that the new interpretation is better than any of the others because it is more complete, has less gaps, is more plausible, etc. Nonetheless he never gets beyond having some more or less adequate, more or less complete human interpretation, and other historians may reject his final assessment as hopelessly biased. And this, I maintain, is simply the human situation. We can only cognize being-as, but we are aware of a reality (Suchness) of which being-as is only a partial clarification or illumination.

One of the difficulties with the Kantian epistemology, to which my own view has obvious affinities, is the unsatisfactory hiatus between phenomena and noumena, concepts and the *Ding an sich*. Of course, there *is* such a distinction, as I have implied all along, but in Kant one gets the false impression that we live entirely within the world of phenomena and concepts, cut off completely from any intercourse with the *Ding an sich*. Noumena, on Kant's view, impinge on ordinary life and thought no more than the average person's awareness of God. He is there somewhere but this has little or no bearing on the person's day-to-day life. But of course this is quite wrong. It is not that there are two kinds of things in the world, phenomena and noumena, and that conceptual thought can only apprehend phenomena. To think is to have a glimpse *of reality*. This is what idealists have always missed. All thought is interpretation, but a more or less *adequate* interpretation *of* reality. We cannot know the thing *in* itself, for this is a contradiction in terms, but we can and do know the *thing itself* in the sense that we perceive aspects *of it* through the projection of meaning.

If we radically separate reality from being-as, reality takes on a mysterious, alien guise, somewhat like Plato's Ideas. But again this is a quite false impression. If I want to indicate what I mean by reality there are at least two courses open to me. First I can simply point to the world beyond; "*That* is what I want to understand, that independent reality out there." In this sense reality is not a mysterious entity on the "other side" of experience, but the most ubiquitous item *in* experience. Secondly I can explain the place of "reality" in our thought and language, showing how we use the concept to mark an awareness of correctible inadequacies in our own views and interpretations, to express our desire to get to the bottom of things, and so on. I set a chair before me and try to describe it. The reality is right there before me, perfectly ordinary, but my description automatically converts it into a projected interpretation through which I am able to understand this humanly understood aspect of the world. The chair does have this aspect and so my interpretation is more or less correct, but its having this aspect does not preclude its having other aspects, and so I can go on to describe it in other, and perhaps for certain purposes, better ways. But I never get beyond some description or other. Does this mean that I don't understand the chair itself? Not at all. Insofar as the interpretation or description is a good one it gives me valuable information about the chair.

It is clear that we need this account of reality to complete our analysis of projection. At first we are inclined to take the naive objectivist view that meaning is identical with (the essence of) the thing. Then we see that this is projection, and we feel that the thing itself is without meaning (Korzybsi, Bergson, Whitehead, "projection is bad"). Then in a conventionalist, idealist reaction we begin to see that meaning just *is* projection (Urban, Gombrich). And here we come very close to the point of view I want to develop. But this is not the whole story. "Being is being-as" is broadly correct, but this must not be taken to mean that all experience is equally clearly understood nor that we have no experience of a reality opposing or transcending our limited experience. We do have experience of something we describe as reality overflowing and escaping our conceptual grasp. "Reality" has a place in our language, even though we have no experience of it in the sense in which we have an experience of an apple. What we need to do, then, is to go beyond and improve upon the conventionalist, idealist position by treating our experience of reality as a refinement of the "Being is being-as" position. And this is made possible by an existentialist analysis of the human situation. The human situation is that we can only think what we can interpret or conceptualize, yet we also feel that there is more to be known, i.e., a clearer, fuller interpretation to be had than we do in fact have. We have, for example, a clear sense of comparing the interpretation with the facts, often finding the interpretation lacking. But this doesn't mean we compare the interpretation with the thing-in-itself. A "fact," as well as an interpretation, is a meaningful item of experience; comparing interpretation to fact is not, therefore, comparing being-as with reality itself, but rather the comparison of two sorts of being-as. The desire to get clearer about X is a desire to improve upon one's grasp of meaningful aspects; it is not a movement from an aspect to the thing-in-itself. The experience of meaninglessness, as we have seen, is not the experience of reality itself, but the breakdown of coherent experience; it is a feeling of anguish at the loss of a world, not a grasp of a transcendent reality.

But these remarks are not intended as an hypothesis about the world, so much as a statement of fact about the limited human standpoint. We are like a man standing before a huge, many-sided, opaque object. We can only see one side at a time, yet we are aware that there is more to it; we can never grasp it all, though we know we can always learn more and more about it. This does not mean that there is a thing-in-itself *behind* experience or that reality is a *composite* of all these aspects; it is simply a statement of how we stand toward reality. "Reality behind experience" is a telling metaphor, but no more. I can point to X in a way which indicates an aspect, however minimally, but also indicates that there is a plurality of possible aspects, all of which are more or less adequate. I point to it meaning "that thing, whatever you may call it or however you may regard it;" it stands over against our interpretations and has a life of its own though we can't say *what* that is without supplying an interpretation. This is the element of realism left out of the idealist account.

In the sense that Suchness marks the awareness that "that thing" is not identical with my interpretations of it, Suchness is primarily an expression of the limits of language and of conceptual thought. The suggestion that, being standpoint-bound, one never apprehends the thing itself is based on a too literal interpretation of words like "interpretation" and "reality." We say we have an "interpretation of reality," and this seems to suggest two distinct entities, the interpretation and the reality. Then, since we can only know interpretations, reality becomes a mysterious entity of which we only know, somehow, that it exists. But this is based on a false view of language. Words like "interpretation" and "reality" are only tools we use to point to certain aspects of the human situation with which we are all familiar but which we cannot satisfactorily explain to ourselves. As St. Augustine said, we all know what time is until we begin to explain it.

I said earlier that the account of nonlinguistic meaning would have an important bearing on the theory of linguistic meaning. We can now begin to see what this is. Words are meaningful, not in the naive correspondence sense of naming or referring to essential properties, but in the sense in which words can be used to illuminate, clarify, articulate or call attention to certain projected aspects of the world (being-as). Language, then, is one of the ways in which we project meaning. When we look at language as ideally mirroring or corresponding to reality, we are led into the sorts of philosophical puzzles and antinomies discussed earlier. But the sense of puzzlement vanishes when we see language being used to illuminate aspects of the world. Difficulties we saw earlier in distinguishing mind and body, reality and interpretation, are due primarily to a faulty theory of language. Words can only point to or suggest, they cannot fix or capture.

This limited function of language has always been at least partially understood by poets and mystics. This is what they mean, for example, when they speak of thoughts which cannot be put into words. Of course, they do not literally mean what they say, for they generally go on at great length to put into words the very thoughts which they maintain can't be expressed. What they mean is that these thoughts cannot be *perfectly adequately* expressed, that we can only hint at them or suggest their beauty or sublimity. It is a statement, in other words, about the limitations of linguistic expression intended primarily to counter the naive correspondence theory of meaning.

Can we express in words, for example, the "essential unity of man and nature?" Well, in one sense we can and have in fact just done so. We have used the concept "unity" to suggest the kind of relation obtaining between what are conventionally designated as "man" and "nature". But this is only a suggestion, it does not finally fix or capture the relation of man to nature. To accept the mystic's idea of "thoughts too deep for words" is not to despise or eschew altogether literary descriptions of religious or philosophic phenomena. Such remarks should be taken rather as a prescription for how to *understand* such descriptions. They are intended as a warning not to understand the words in a literal, correspondence sense but rather as tools for suggesting to a responsive mind the kind of relation revealed in certain types of religious experience.

Similarly, the Hindu and Buddhist denial that there exists anything in the world—whether minds, objects, thoughts or properties. What is meant, I suggest, is that there is nothing in the world corresponding exactly to human concepts and categories of thought, not that the world is empty in the sense in which a clear sky is void of objects and differentiation. This is what Nan-Chuan was getting at when he wrote,

During the period before the world was manifested there were no names. The moment Buddha (mind) arrives in the world there are names, and so we clutch hold of forms ... . If there are names, everything is classified in limits and bounds.[9]

Also, in Indian thought, the emptiness of *rupa* (things) is a reflection of the conceptual character of *nama* (names), and the illusion of *Maya* is the illusion of the non-projective identification of *nama* and *rupa*. This is less a metaphysical assertion about the nature of reality (that it is void) than an assertion of the limitations of language. As such it is a denial, not of the existence of things, but of reified concepts. It is less a theory of reality than a theory of language, a warning not to mistake the finger for the moon, the concept for the object. As Huang-Po says,

[9] Nan-Ch'uan, in: Watts, Allen, *The Way of Zen*, New York: Mentor Books, 1959. p. 129.

Men are afraid to forget their own minds, fearing to fall through the void with nothing on to which they can cling. They do not know that the void is not really the void but the real realm of the Dharma [things.] [10]

As we saw in the case of Heidegger, the assertion of emptiness is not a denial that things exist in the world, but an assertion of the emptiness *of* these things. It is not an attempt to "wipe them out," but to point out something about them, namely, that they are in themselves void of the meanings we attach to them, and in this sense empty, i.e., devoid of human significance. In the end we get the world back exactly as it was before, though our understanding of it is profoundly different. As Huang-Po puts it, "Who told you to eliminate anything? Look at the void in front of your eyes. How can you produce it or eliminate it?" [11]

Historically this was a practical problem of textual interpretation in the instruction of young Buddhist monks. The sacred texts typically asserted that things were unreal, that any duality was illusory, and then went on to prescribe various techniques for eliminating all such discriminating thought—polishing the mirror, as it was called, wiping it clean, so that it would reflect everything and retain nothing. But understood in a literal, correspondence way, as a metaphysical theory of reality, such assertions are complete nonsense and lead to a quiescent state of self-hypnotic tranquillity to which later Mahayanist and especially Japanese Zen thought was diametrically opposed. The corrective to this omnipresent source of misunderstanding was to interpret the emptiness of things as the emptiness of reified concepts, to realize the projective nature of thought without thereby *altering* ordinary thought or the world of ordinary experience. As Seng-Chao writes,

When we say that there is neither existence nor non-existence, does it mean to wipe out all the myriad things, blot out our seeing and hearing, and be in a state without sound, form or substance before we can call it absolute truth? Truly, [absolute truth] is in accord with things as they are and therefore is opposed to none .... Not being existent and not being non-existent do not mean that there are no things, but that all things are not things in the real [nonprojective] sense. As all things are not things in the

---

[10] Huang-Po, *The Teaching of Huang Po* (John Blofeld, trans.), New York: Grove Press, 1959, p. 41.

[11] *Ibid.*, p. 53.

real sense, what is there in relation to which a thing can be so-called? Therefore the scripture says, 'Matter is empty by virtue of its own nature; it is not empty because it has been destroyed.' [12]

There *are* things and they are empty. Insofar as we project meanings, there is a diversified world of objects and multiple distinctions. In a sense, everything is as it was before—except, of course, ourselves, who no longer accept the givenness of this world naively. We are not to deny or destroy this world, but simply to *see* that it *is* a projection, that in themselves there are no conceptual categories exactly corresponding with reality, but only human concepts we use for our own ends to differentiate the world into individual, self-contained entities. Thus, when Huang-Po writes, "There is no 'self' and no 'other.' There is no 'wrong desire,' no 'anger,' no 'hatred,' no 'love,' no 'victory,' no 'failure'," [13] we must be careful how we understand him. In one sense the assertion is true; but in another sense, of course, it is quite false. *Of course*, there is hatred, love and failure in the world. If our understanding of language views words like "hatred," "love," and "failure" as illuminating certain genuine aspects of the world from different human standpoints, then it is obviously *true* to say that there *is* hatred, love and failure. But if we view language as naming essential attributes, i.e., as literally corresponding with objects, then it would be *false* to say that hatred, love and failure exist in our world. The assertion that there is no hatred or failure is the assertion that hatred and failure are to be viewed, not as things in the world, but as concepts we use with varying degrees of success to illuminate certain aspects of the world.

Since religious instruction, like all instruction, must rely on linguistic media, there is a persistent danger of misunderstanding which a great deal of Zen writing is designed to correct. This difficulty is unavoidable insofar as it is built into the very nature of language. As language philosophers have said more recently, the very form of words we use is misleading. To express the fact that men mistake concepts for reality, classical Buddhists texts contrasted ignorance with enlightenment, the emptiness of reality with the fullness of things in the ordinary world of appearances. But this immediately suggests some special state of mind to be achieved, namely, enlighten-

---

[12] Seng-Chao, "The Emptiness of the Unreal," in: *A Source Book in Chinese Philosophy* (Wing-Tsit Chan, ed. and trans.), Princeton: Princeton University Press, 1963, p. 353.

[13] Huang-Po, *op. cit.*, p. 88.

ment, and that this enlightenment consists in the realization that the world is comprised of the sole and unusual property of being utterly empty. But this is the very way of thinking the texts sought to overcome.

Some of the most puzzling comments in the Zen literature are concerned with eliminating this constant source of misunderstanding. As Huang-Po says,

There *are* no enlightened men or ignorant men, and there *is* no oblivion. Yet though basically everything is without objective existence, you must not come to think in terms of anything non-existent; and though things are not non-existent, you must not form a concept of anything existing. For 'existence' and 'non-existence' are both empirical concepts no better than illusions.[14]

It is not a question of asserting or denying objects or properties in the world; it is primarily a question of how we understand the words we do use to describe the objects we do experience. "Oblivion" and "emptiness" are concepts we use to suggest the projective nature of thought and the being-as character of things in the world of ordinary experience. These are useful devices and properly understood lead to true assertions about reality, but, contrary to their intended meaning, they also tend to suggest the false position that there exists a special state of mind in which reality is apprehended as blank oblivion.

As Wittgenstein said at the end of the *Tractatus*, we are forced to use language in an attempt to overcome the misleading implications of language.[15] The Zen writer is using language to lead us out of a false view of language, though everything he says can be understood, and more easily understood, in the old, misleading way. Once we have overcome this false view of language, we are free to speak about the world as we always have. But we understand these expressions now in a radically new light.

Similarly, in the classic negative path of mystic writers. Reality, it is said, is not A or B or C or anything else you care to mention. If we understand such expressions as denying these features of reality in the naive objectivist or correspondence sense, we come up with the preposterous interpretation that reality is a formless void in the

[14] *Ibid.*, p. 68.

[15] Wittgenstein, Ludwig, *Tractatus Logico-Philosophicus* (D. F. Pears and B. F. McGuinness, trans.), London: Routledge and Kegal Paul 1963, pp. 145-151.

light of which ordinary experience is a complete and utter illusion. But if we view such statements as putting forward one view of language at the expense of another, then they begin to make sense. Reality is not A in the sense that A does not fix or exhaust reality; A is a human interpretation which clarifies for us certain facets of reality from our point of view, but does not objectively *belong* to or *correspond* with that reality. As Huang-Po puts it, reality

is not green nor yellow and has neither form nor appearance. It does not belong to the categories of things which exist or do not exist .... It is neither long nor short, big nor small, for it transcends all limits, measures, names, traces and comparisons. It is that which you see before you [Suchness]—begin to reason about it and you at once fall into error. It is *like* the boundless void which cannot be fathomed or measured.[16]

The point is not that we can't meaningfully and truly make comparisons and draw distinctions, which we obviously can, but that reality "transcends all names and comparisons." The error is in reifying concepts, that is, naively projecting meaning without being aware that one is doing so. As Ho-Yen says,

Tao has no name .... It is clear that to give a name perforce is merely to give an appellation on the basis only of what people know.[17]

This is why most mystic writers eventually express themselves in terms of nonduality. This may be formulated, "It is neither X nor not X, nor is it neither X nor non-X nor both X and non-X; but we use the term 'X' to call attention to it." As Nagarjuna put it,

It cannot be called void or not void,
Or both or neither;
But in order to point it out,
It is called 'the Void'.[18]

This has the advantage of exhausting every conventional interpretation in terms of existence or nonexistence, and thereby eliminating the source of misunderstanding. Putting it this way attacks head-on the conventional, objectivist understanding of the relation of word to

16 Huang-Po, *op. cit.*, p. 29 (my italics).
17 Ho-Yen, "Treatise on the Nameless," in: *A Source Book in Chinese Philosophy*, *op. cit.*, p. 325.
18 Nagarjuna, *Madhyamika Shastra*, in: Zimmer, Heinrich, *Philosophies of India*, New York: Meridian Books, 1957, p. 521; cf. "Examination of Nirvana," in: *The Teaching of the Compassionate Buddha* (E. A. Burtt, ed.), New York: A Mentor Book, 1955, pp. 172-175.

object, frustrating it and putting it, at least temporarily, in abeyance, so that one is prepared to understand in a radically new way the idea that we "use the term to call attention to it." As Huang-Po says, "it is *like* the boundless void." We use the idea of the void, not to deny the multiplicity of things in the world, but to call attention to the fact that the lines of demarcation between things are lines we have traced from our own point of view for our own purposes. The lines are there to be traced, so to speak, but they are not traced until we trace them.

So let your symbolic conception be that of a void … . Eschew all symbolizing whatever, for by this eschewal is 'symbolized' the Great Void in which is neither unity nor multiplicity—that Void which is not really void, that Symbol which is no symbol.[19]

It is like trying to draw a picture of a tree. There are many aspects of the tree which may interest us and which we can convey with varying degrees of success by lines drawn on paper. We may be impressed with the overall configurations of the leafy section of the tree which we may translate as a single linear outline. Or, we may be interested in the relation of light to darker areas which we transcribe onto paper as black and white patches. These aspects are there to be drawn, but it is we who emphasize them by drawing them, calling attention to them. There *is* a shape to the tree which some outlines convey better than others, but no single continuous line tracing this. There *are* lighter and darker areas, but no patches of black and white.

Another stratagem devised by later Buddhist writers to get round such misunderstandings was to interpret the classic texts as tools or devices for getting the uninitiated from a naive way of looking at things to a more sophisticated standpoint. In Chi-Tsang those on the first level ordinarily suppose objects exist just as they appear to us, and the classic texts, addressing themselves to *this* level of thought, begin by showing reasons why these objects do *not* exist in this way. These arguments lead to a kind of idealism in which phenomenal objects are said to be unreal and only Mind (Buddha) is real. But this second stage of awareness is only intended as a device to get the initiates away from a naive absorption in things; it is not meant, in this literal sense, to characterize the final Buddhist position. And so, comes the third and final stage in which it becomes clear that all these terms, "reality," "emptiness," "duality," are

[19] Huang-Po, *op. cit.*, pp. 122-123.

simply devices for overcoming a false view of the relation of thought to reality. As Chi-Tsang puts it,

Ordinary people say that dharmas [things] ... possess being, without realizing that they possess nothing. Therefore, the Buddhas propound to them the doctrine that dharmas are ultimately empty and void. When it is said that dharmas [things] possess being, it is ordinary people who say so. This is worldly truth, the truth of ordinary people ... . Next comes the second stage, which explains that both being and non-being belong to worldly truth, whereas non-duality (neither being nor non-being) belongs to absolute truth ... . Next comes the third stage in which both duality and non-duality are worldly truths.[20]

And elsewhere,

The idea of non-existence is presented primarily to handle the disease of the concept of existence. If that disease disappears, the useless medium is also discarded ... . We are forced to use the word 'correct' in order to stop the perverseness. Once perverseness has been stopped, correctness will no longer remain.[21]

And in *The Chung Lun,*

The Great Sage preached the law of Emptiness
In order to free men from all views.
If one still holds the view that Emptiness exists,
Such a person the Buddhas will not transform.[22]

As Wittgenstein said in the *Tractatus*, philosophic language is like a ladder for extracting ourselves from the pit of a naive view of language. Once we have climbed out, we no longer need the ladder.[23] ("When the fish is caught, we pay no more attention to the trap" —a traditional Zen saying.) [24]

On the third level one sees assertions about the being of Nirvana, Buddha, etc., and the nonbeing of duality, objects, etc., as statements about the nature of thought and language and their relation to reality. If we are aware that thought and language are the projection of human concepts and meanings, then, coming full circle, there is no danger, and hence nothing false in saying that the world is full of different individual things. There is no denial of anything in the

---

[20] Chi-Tsang, in: *A Source Book in Chinese Philosophy, op. cit.,* p. 360.

[21] *Ibid.,* p. 366.

[22] Nagarjuna, *Madhyamika Shastra,* quoted by Chi-Tsang from the Chinese translation, *The Chung Lun,* in: *A Source Book in Chinese Philosophy, op. cit.,* p. 367.

[23] Wittgenstein, *op. cit.,* p. 151.

[24] In: Huang-Po, *op. cit.,* p. 55.

world, only various attempts to correct inadequate ideas as to how we stand toward things in the world. The important thing is to see what words can be made to do and what they cannot be made to do.

Even Enlightenment, the Absolute, Reality, Sudden Attainment, the Dharmakaya and all the others ... are—everyone of them—mere concepts for helping us through samsara, they have nothing to do with the real Buddha-Mind.[25]

'Studying the Way' is just a figure of speech ... . Studying leads to the retention of concepts and so the way is entirely misunderstood ... . The first step is to refrain from knowledge-based concepts ... . You must not allow this name ('Way') to lead you into forming a mental concept of a road.[26]

Are there objects and properties in the world? In one sense, according to one view of language and meaning (projection), yes; in another sense, according to another view of language and meaning (naive objectivist, or correspondence), no. The wisdom of Zen writing is its keen awareness of this ambiguity. In the end, as Wittgenstein also said in *Philosophical Investigations*, nothing is denied, everything is "given back," and we return to square one.[27] As Ch'ing-Yuan has beautifully expressed it,

Before I had studied Zen for thirty years, I saw mountains as mountains, and waters as waters. When I arrived at a more intimate knowledge, I came to the point where I saw that mountains are not mountains, and waters are not waters. But now that I have got its very substance I am at rest. For its just that I see mountains once again as mountains, and waters once again as waters.[28]

This is also very much Husserl's approach, as mentioned earlier. We begin by supposing that objects are simply identical with our way of describing them. We naively accept a meaningful world of projected meanings. Later we see that these meanings are projected and this leads to the idealist denial that there *are* any mountains, etc., in

---

[25] Huang Po, *Ibid.*, p. 69.

[26] *Ibid.*, pp. 54-55; cf. Wittgenstein, Ludwig, "A *picture* held us captive. And we could not get outside it, for it lay in our language and language seemed to repeat it to us inexorably," in: *Philosophical Investigations* (G. E. M. Anscombe, trans.), New York: The Macmillan Company, 1953, p. 48.

[27] Wittgenstein, *Ibid.*, pp. 47-52; cf. Nagarjuna, "Nothing is abandoned, nothing annihilated," in: Zimmer, *op. cit.*, p. 518.

[28] Ch'ing-Yuan, in: Watts, *op. cit.*, p. 127.

reality. But this is simply the opposite side of the naive objectivist sense of meaning, which is logically inconsistent. It does not follow that we do not live in a meaningful world of being-as. And so we are led to a final assessment which neither denies nor affirms, but simply takes note of the projective nature of meaning and the being-as character of the world. Naively, mountains just are mountains. But this naive view is wrong; mountains are not *simply* mountains, that is, reality is not exhausted by but overflows our concept of "mountain," and in this sense, mountains are *not* mountains. But once we have got beyond this naive view of meaning, we are free to say once again that in the sense that "mountain" does illuminate a perceptible aspect of the world from a certain point of view, mountains *are* mountains. In the end we live in a meaningful world of projected meanings *knowing* they are projections and valuing them nonetheless for that.

In much the same way the poet's hesitation in accepting a critic's interpretation of his poetry expresses more an uneasiness over the limitations of critical discourse than a dissatisfaction with any particular interpretation. Robert Frost was frequently asked on his university tours whether his poem "Stopping by Woods on a Snowy Evening" had anything to do with death. In particular he was asked whether the last lines of the poem,

And miles to go before I sleep,
And miles to go before I sleep.,

meant that the desirability of death was offset by the more onerous responsibilities in the here and now.[29] To which Frost invariably replied "no." The poem, he said, described a man stopping briefly in his carriage to view a snow-filled wood before continuing on to town. Similarly, Picasso reportedly replied to a critic that his painting of a red bull's head was *not* a portrait of Facism, but simply a picture of a red bull.

On the one hand we can appreciate this chary attitude; on the other hand, it seems more than a little disingenuous. In one sense Frost's poem *is* about death; but of course it is not *just* the assertion that the desirability of death is offset by one's responsibility to the living, an interpretation the poet is naturally and rightly anxious to disown.

[29] Frost, Robert, "Stopping by Woods on a Snowy Evening," in: *Robert Frost's Poems* (Louis Untermeyer, ed.), New York: Pocket Books, Inc., p. 194.

The prose statement of the meaning of a poem is not and cannot be
identical with the meaning of the poem itself. Otherwise, we could
take the prose statement and dispense with the poem. In this sense,
as is often said, form and content in poetry are one. Change the form
of words and you change the meaning. In this sense one cannot
"say" what a poem means, and this often prompts the assertion that
poems don't have any meaning at all ("A poem should not mean,/
But be.") [30]

But in another sense we obviously *can* "say" what a poem or a line
of poetry means, and so the dispute is really over the sense in which
one can and cannot "say what a poem means." It is more a concern
with the nature of language than of poetry. If we think of language
as mirroring the real world, as the identity of word and object in
the naive objectivist sense, then in *that* sense one can*not* say what a
poem means, just as one cannot say in *that* sense what anything
means. But if we think of language as calling attention to certain
aspects of things by hints and suggestions, then one obviously *can*
say what a poem means. At least we can place the meaning within
certain limits on which most of us can agree. Frost's poem has
something to do with death, nihilism or *something of the sort*. The
words "death," "repose," "renunciation," "nihilism" are more apt,
or more indicative than words like "frenzy" or "horror." We use the
former to bring someone to see for himself that unique meaning of
the poem which cannot be spelled out completely in any translation.
A poem is untranslatable then in the sense that no translation fixes
or captures its meaning once and for all or is substitutible for it.
Once we see the limitations of translations and critical interpretations
we may proceed to Ch'ing-Yuan's third stage and continue to translate
and offer interpretations—knowing now what we are doing and what
we are not; aware, that is, of the sense in which poems can be translated and the sense in which they cannot. In the language of the
Tractatus we cannot "say" what a poem means we can only "show" it;
but then, carefully examined, we realize that nothing can be "said"
in this literal sense.

Our concern, then, is primarily one of linguistic meaning. In the
naive objectivist or correspondence sense of meaning, projection
implies that things are simply meaningless; but in the sense that

[30] Macleish, Archibald, "Ars Poetica," in: *Collected Poems 1917-1952*, Boston:
Houghton Mifflin Company, 1952, p. 41.

words and concepts can illuminate certain facets of reality from limited human points of view, things are meaningful. This theory of language and meaning, only vaguely suggested in mystical and critical literature, is worked out in both depth and detail in Heidegger's interpretation of the unveiling function of truth.

We have already examined Heidegger's view, in his analysis of "Being-in-the-world," that thought, and indeed human existence, presupposes an already meaningful world of interpreted, previously understood objects. As he says, we always and necessarily stand both "in truth" and "in untruth." [31] That is, as human beings we find ourselves in an environment of partially understood entities which we may proceed to clarify or articulate in a more intellectually rigorous or explicit form. Putting it the other way round, whatever we theoretically conclude about the world is a refinement or articulation of what has already been intuitively perceived in "non-thematic circumspection," that unreflexive, absorbed understanding of things which Heidegger calls fore-conception.[32]

Language, on this view, is primarily a disclosing or revealing of various aspects of reality. It is only after habitual usage has frozen certain forms of speech into cliches that we lose sight of this revelatory feature of language and come eventually to view language as literally mirroring or corresponding to objects in the world. The naive, every-day absorption in nonprojective meaning is especially disclosure-blind in this sense.

Traditional philosophy presupposes this degenerate, disclosure-blind level of thought and operates always within this naive stand-point, inquiring, for example, whether given interpretations match given facts and ignoring *how* we come by these facts and interpretations in the first place, Heidegger tries to re-open the discussion of truth on the more fundamental plane of man's basic projecting nature. This suggests the very close relation in Heidegger, not only of meaning and Being (being-as), but of meaning and truth as well. In both meaning is basic. As human beings we live in an interpreted world of meaningful items cohering in a more or less intelligible system. This is what makes Being and truth possible. Because I see that as a chair or a pencil the world is not empty but has content (Being or

---

[31] Heidegger, Martin, *Being and Time* (John Macquarrie and Edward Robinson, trans.), London: S.C.M. Press, 1962, pp. 263-264.
[32] *Ibid.*, pp. 107, 191.

being-as), and it is also because of this that I am able to truly think
and say "That is a chair," "That is a pencil." As Heidegger says,

All interpretation is grounded on understanding. That which has been
articulated as such in interpretation and sketched out before-hand in the
understanding ... is the meaning. In so far as assertion ('judgment') is
grounded on understanding and presents us with a derivative form in which
an interpretation has been carried out, it *too* has a meaning.[33]

Truth and Being, for Heidegger, rest on humanly projected meaning. To be human is to project meaning, and to project meaning is
to make possible being-as (Being); this in turn provides the most
basic form of truth from which more sophisticated forms arise.
Spoken language, then, gives expression to some prior way of understanding, bringing it to light, articulating and then preserving what
is already in some sense cognized. The point of descriptive discourse,
therefore, is not to name the essential properties of objects (i.e., not
truth in the naive correspondence sense), but communication, that is,
to bring the hearer to the speaker's point of view, to illuminate for
the hearer the aspect intended by the speaker, to get the hearer into
position to see this aspect for himself. Communication, for Heidegger,
is "aimed at bringing the hearer to participate in disclosed Being
towards what is talked about in the discourse." [34]

Truth, then, on Heidegger's view, is primarily a kind of interpretation possible only within projective human thought.

Dasein, as constituted by disclosedness, is essentially in the truth. Disclosedness is a kind of Being which is essential to *Dasein*. *'There is' truth
only in so far as* Dasein *is and so long as* Dasein *is*. Entities are uncovered
only *when* Dasein *is*; and only as long as Dasein *is*, are they disclosed.[35]

Truth is fundamentally the revelation of projected meaning, the
illumination of reality as being-as (Being). Again, the very close
proximity between Being and truth, resting, in the final analysis,
on Heidegger's theory of meaning. "Being (not entities) is something
'there is' only in so far as truth is, and truth *is* only in so far as and
as long as *Dasein* is. Being and truth 'are' equiprimordially." [36]

Thus, thought and language can never do more than point to

---

[33] *Ibid.*, p. 195.
[34] *Ibid.*, p. 212.
[35] *Ibid.*, p. 269.
[36] *Ibid.*, p. 272.

reality; they cannot capture or fix it in the nonprojective sense. Once we thoroughly grasp this point we are free to accept and describe a meaningful world of humanly disclosed, projected meanings. Thus, we reject the tragic sense of meaninglessness by affirming the essentially projecting nature of thought and language.

And so, in a sense we return to square one. A naive acceptance of nonprojective meaning leads to a sense of meaninglessness. At first we blindly accept a nonprojection sense of meaning. But then *because* of this objectivist criterion of meaning, the realization that meaning is projection carries with it the implication that there is no *non*projected meaning and hence *no* meaning at all. But now rejecting this nonprojection ideal of meaning as gratuitous and contradictory, we see that projection *guarantees* meaning and the world once again becomes meaningful. These are precisely the three stages referred to in Ch'ing-Yuan's statement above. At first, we see mountains as mountains, then we come to the point where we see that mountains are not mountains, and finally we return to the position in which mountains once again are mountains.

But, of course, this is *not quite* a return to square one. On the first level we are naively, that is, blindly, absorbed in projection. We mistake the finger for the moon; we fail to distinguish the object from the way in which we cognize it. This is what leads to the tragic sense of meaninglessness. On the third level we knowingly accept projection. We acknowledge what we have been doing all along, projecting a meaningful world of disclosed being-as. On the first level there is no appreciation of man's essential projecting nature or the being-as nature of the world, or of Suchness transcending human thought. On the third level we can appreciate the way in which projection reveals aspects of reality without "mirroring" reality and, on the other side, we gain a sense of a reality which can be pointed to but never "captured."

And this is precisely what we as human beings are free to do—acknowledge our own projecting nature. We are compelled to project meaning, but we are free to recognize and accept the fact that it is our nature to do so. This is the key to the paradox of freedom in Heidegger. How is one free to accept or reject his own *nature*? Similarly the Buddhist paradox how one can become what one already is (the Buddha). It is our nature to form concepts, demarcate, delineate, measure, distinguish—in a word, to project meaning, to illuminate

being-as. We can do nothing about this. But we are free to acknowledge this fact and own up to it.

But this means that we are free to reject as alien to ourselves
absorption, attachment and fallenness, and since it is precisely this
naive absorption which leads to meaninglessness in the tragic sense,
we are free, finally, to reject the tragic sense of meaninglessness.

BIBLIOGRAPHY

Adamov, Arthur, "The Endless Humiliation" (Richard Howard, trans.).
  Evergreen Review, vol. 2, no. 8, 1959.
—, *L'Invasion*, in *Théâtre*, vol. 1. Paris: Gallimard, 1953.
Beckett, Samuel, *Waiting for Godot*. London: Faber and Faber, 1959.
Bergson, Henri, *An Introduction to Metaphysics* (T. E. Hulme, trans.).
  New York: Liberal Arts, 1949.
Camus, Albert, *The Myth of Sisyphus* (Justin O'Brien, trans.). New York:
  Vintage Books, 1960.
Chan, Wing-tsit, trans., *A Source Book of Chinese Philosophy*. Princeton:
  Princeton University Press, 1963.
Coe, Richard N., *Ionesco*. London: Oliver and Boyd, 1961.
Dewey, John, *Reconstruction in Philosophy*. New York: Mentor, 1950.
Esslin, Martin, *The Theatre of the Absurd*. Harmondsworth, England:
  Penguin Books, 1968.
Evans-Pritchard, Edward, *Social Anthropology*. London: Cohen and West,
  1951.
Frankfort, H., *et al.*, *Before Philosophy*. Harmondsworth, England: Penguin
  Books, 1951.
Heidegger, Martin, *Being and Time* (John McQuarrie and Edward Robin-
  son, trans.). London: S. C. M. Press, 1962.
Huang-po, *The Teaching of Huang Po* (John Blofeld, trans.). New York:
  Grove, 1959.
Husserl, Edmund, *The Idea of Phenomenology* (William Alston and George
  Nakhnikian, trans.). The Hague: Martinus Nijhoff, 1964.
Ionesco, Eugene, *Fragments of a Journal* (Jean Stewart, trans.). New York:
  Grove, 1968.
—, "Point of Departure" (L. C. Pronko, trans.). *Theatre Arts*, vol. 42,
  no. 6, 1958.
Kant, Immanuel, *Critique of Judgment* (Bernard, trans.). New York:
  Hafner, 1951.
King, Magda, *Heidegger's Philosophy*. New York: Dell, 1964.
Levi-Straus, Claude, *Structural Anthropology* (Jacobson and Schoepf,
  trans.). New York: Basic Books, 1963.
Nietzsche, Friedrich, *The Will to Power* (A. M. Ludovici, trans.) in *The*

Complete Works of Friedrich Nietzsche (Oscar Levi, ed.), vol. 15. New York: Russell and Russell, 1964.

Radhakrishnan, Sarvepalli and Charles Moore, ed., *A Source Book in Indian Philosophy*. Princeton: Princeton University Press, 1957.

Richards, I. A. and C. K. Ogden, *The Meaning of Meaning*. London: Routledge and Kegan Paul, 1956.

Sartre, Jean-Paul, *Being and Nothingness* (H. E. Barnes, trans.). New York; Philosophical Library, 1956.

—, "Existentialism and Humanism," in Morton White (ed.), *The Age of Reason*. New York: Mentor, 1955.

—, *Nausea* (Lloyd Alexander, trans.). Norfolk, Conn.: New Directions, 1959.

Suzuki, D. T., *Zen Buddhism* (William Barrett, ed.). Garden City: Doubleday, 1956.

Watts, Alan, *The Way of Zen*. New York: Mentor, 1957.

Whitehead, Alfred N., *Science and the Modern World*. New York: Mentor, 1958.

Wittgenstein, Ludwig, *Philosophical Investigations* (G. E. M. Anscombe, trans.). New York: Macmillan, 1953.

—, *Remarks on the Logical Foundations of Mathematics* (G. E. M. Anscombe, trans.). Cambridge, Mass.: M.I.T. Press, 1967.

—, *Tractatus Logico-philosophicus*. London: Kegan Paul, 1922.

INDEX

Abraham, W.   47, 48
Adamov   23, 24, 38, 107, 108, 114
Alston, W.   1, 2, 6
Aristotle   51, 53, 54, 60, 73
Austin   87
Ayer   67

Beckett   18, 24, 97, 99, 108, 118
Bergson   53, 57-59, 125
Berkeley   xii, 57
Blackman, H. J.   29
Bradley   54
Burnet, J.   53, 54

Camus   18, 21, 22, 28, 44, 104-106,
   108, 114
Chi-tsang   133, 134
Ching-yuan   135-137, 140
Coe, Richard   19, 107, 116
Coleridge   x, 30, 43, 80, 81, 117
Comte   49

Descartes   60, 61, 63
Dewey   50, 53, 70
Dilman, Ilham   14-17, 22

Esslin, Martin   18, 24, 108, 114
Evans-Pritchard   6

Genet   25-27, 45

Hegel   53, 55
Heidegger   x, xii, 13, 25, 29-31, 39-41,
   60, 68-72, 91-96, 99, 102, 110, 111,
   118, 119-121, 138-140

Ho-yen   132
Huang-po   128-133, 135
Husserl   68-70, 86, 119, 120, 135

Ionesco   x, 18-20, 23, 26, 35, 97, 98,
   106, 107, 114, 116, 118

Jaspers   110

Kant   12, 13, 19, 31, 53, 104, 123-125
Korzybski   85, 117, 123, 125

Leibniz   13, 52, 79
Levi-Straus   6
Locke   89

Mounier   109, 111

Nagarjuna   132, 134
Nan-ch'uan   128
Newton   51, 52, 79, 81
Nietzsche   44, 45, 59, 82-85, 111, 117

Parmenides   54, 112
Pascal   22
Plato   13, 52-57, 60, 61, 82, 125

Rankin, K. W.   6-8, 44
Richards, I. A.   x, 1, 2, 6, 36, 37, 41,
   78
Rickman, H. P.   9, 11, 44
Rilke   80
Russell   64
Ryle   60, 70

Santayana 56, 61, 82
Sartre 12, 13, 18, 20, 22, 25-28, 35,
   45, 77, 101, 102, 106, 108, 109, 111
Schelling 81
Seng-chao 129
Strawson 60

Tolstoy 16

Urban, W. 123, 126

Watts 100
Whitehead 48, 50, 56, 57, 61, 82, 125
Wild 29, 30, 44, 103
Wisdom 66, 67
Wittgenstein x, 8-10, 13, 16, 41, 64-
   67, 131, 134, 135
Wordsworth 80, 81

8655